TotallyU: A Source of Truth

A Career Professional's State of Mind in the Pursuit of Meaning

Gaile G. Sweeney

Published by Gaile Sweeney, LLC, 2022.

TOTALLYU: A SOURCE OF TRUTH

First edition. March 26, 2022.

ISBN: 978-0578916484

Written by Gaile G. Sweeney.

Also by Gaile G. Sweeney

A Career Professional's State of Mind in the Pursuit of Meaning
TotallyU: A Source of Truth

To my mother

"In time everything will be beautiful," —Selfin Sweeney (RIP)

TotallyU: A Source of Truth

TotallyU: A Source of Truth

A Career Professional's State of Mind in the Pursuit of Meaning

Gaile Sweeney

Copyright

First Printing: 2022

Gaile Sweeney, LLC

Coconut Creek, FL 33073

www.gailesweeney.com

Optional Ordering Information:

Special discounts are available on quantity purchases by corporations, associations, educators, and others.

For details, contact the publisher at the above-listed address.

Email info@gailesweeney.com

ISBN: 978-0-578-91648-4

Dedication

To my mother

"In time everything will be beautiful,"—Selfin Sweeney (RIP)

Acknowledgment

———

F aced with the daunting responsibility of the message I wanted to
send out into the world, it took me four years to finish writing this
book. The contents come from the conversations I had with different
versions of myself as I attempted to make sense of my career trajectory
and the loyalty to my other versions of me. Time has allowed me to
gain clarity, recreate and reinvent. As a result, I write my career message
to present to fellow career professionals in what I hope is an engaging
and relatable way.

Over the years, I'm honored to have received a heavy dose of
encouragement and support from the many people who reached out
to me, all searching for hope. I work from a privileged position as I
share their journeys and prior experiences of unresponsive recruiters,
micromanager bosses, low-value job descriptions, poor salaries, and
career burnout. Their challenges, conversations, and solutions have
marked the start of their journey as I peel back layers in my own life,
making room for deep introspection, experience, knowledge and
understanding fuses. Sometimes life is not about letting go; it is simply
engaging others in conversations outside of their heads. Often these are
conversations that may not be so pleasant, yet wholly necessary and,
once faced, totally navigable.

Along the way, like an empty vessel waiting to fill and a sponge, I have
soaked up the encouragement to advocate and guide by watching and
learning. I am thankful to God for my faith, and I am grateful He uses
me as a vessel and places His message and trust in me. Like many, I've
suffered professionally, and I've put bandages on the wounds from the
losses I gambled. We all face responsibilities and make mistakes, or life
just happens. And by human default, instead of being compassionate

with ourselves, we become judgmental of the current situation and lack of progress, and we end up self-sabotaging ourselves with pity. Hence, I never judge.

I provide workable solutions for 'stuck' career professionals with no growth. These individuals remind me of how much satisfaction I get from empowering people. For career professionals who feel undervalued, stuck, and at a disadvantage, we are all in this together. We can achieve the best result from interaction by trusting our vulnerabilities with each other. Thank you for jumping in with encouraging words from the earliest stages of this project to completion. Your experiences shared provide many of my scripted stories.

I am a huge apostle for thanking, and I hope I do not ruin the gesture of embellishing my gratitude to those I interviewed while researching content for this book. I met with the homeless who had fallen from the top of the corporate ladder, the very successful, and those individuals merely trying to get by. And the biggest takeaway from these encounters? There is no difference between an individual standing in the corporate pyramid and the everyday person struggling to survive daily. We all struggle at some point in our careers, and as we evolve, so does the organizational systems and the technology revolutionizes. Some of us give in, some of us face it, while the others ride along on the tides.

Joining me on this journey is my father, my Papa Rock, my motivator, my "why" in everything I do. Each time I remember the sacrifices he made for me to have a future with opportunities to write this book, I wonder how I was delivering my message and making him proud of his legacy. Because of you, Papa, I could see the future.

We all want at least one thing to improve at work, at home, or any other aspect of life so we can leave our world a better place for those that follow us. We get wiser in our pursuit to figure out our career and life. We either pile up and let the critical part of the career dream we once have escape or we negotiate with life to get the job we want right now. For some of us, we would rather take the optimistic path. We'd gather the lessons from our experiences and move on without bitterness.

Introduction

———

We spend a fortune on the degrees and certificates plastered on our walls, and they tell a story. They say we are achievers, we have tenacity, and we're committed, yet, for some of us, the trajectory of our professional journey says otherwise. We're led to believe success is supposed to increase steadily, yet we all want things to be different. We'd like to improve at work, at home, and within many other aspects of life, not just for us, but so we can also leave the world, and our universe, a slightly better place than how we found it. Nonetheless, the moment we start working, a repetitive career cycle begins—merging the psychological construct of the human mind and the mutual dependencies with organizational entities at different points of our career cycle.

In our pursuit to figure out our career, subconsciously, we acquire the state of mind of what I call an *Achiever*, *Drifter*, or *Defeater* as we strive to find existence, meaning, and importance in our work environment. Scientific appropriations on different degrees of validity and accuracy do not medicate our reality. We pile up life with meaningless 'stuff' to get the job we want right now whilst letting the critical part of our career dream we once had escape. This experience can throw us into emotional disarray and confusion regarding how we think, feel, respond, and perform in the workplace. But this is not inevitable. The aim is to avoid surrender.

We have a total responsibility to ourselves rather than have others view us as passive recipients who unintentionally act on impulses to make sense of the career cycle we find ourselves within. Before we proactively fuel our desire for actual success and chase a well-functioning desired path, we need to understand the psychological and physiological mastery of this resilience. And to do so involves a step-by-step process of owning our truth and reframing our state of mind to experience the change at any given stage within the career cycle.

Given the ongoing labor market globalization, fragmented job choices, work instability, and forced occupational mobility, personal concerns about status control may override the concerns that remain within our control. The relationship between what we cannot control, and our emotional triggers are most important to our psychological safety at work and central to our job performance. This exact connection is the reason why I conceived the *Totally^U Framework* as a concept to encompass our employment experiences constructively.

The *Totally^U* concept emphasizes where you identify yourself within the stage of the career cycle, either at the *Achiever, Drifter*, or *Defeater Stage*. The *Totally^U Framework* solidifies any self-change constructive strategy that preserves your whole being and professional career identity. The *U* embraces an exponential function for the infinite possibilities of your career dreams, describing your growth or decay at each stage of the *Totally^U Career Cycle*. Therefore, the *Totally^U Framework* embraces career shifts and status adjustments for those:

- who do not experience emotional discomfort,
- do not need to change but want to, and
- those who desire meaningfulness and are ready to shift positions within the *Career Cycle*.

This deflection produces positive and negative emotional thoughts, feelings, and behaviors as the *Cycle* turns. These emotional states are necessary to motivate our self-regulated interpersonal *burners* away from one stage to a more desired stage within the *Career Cycle*. With a high level of accountability and commitment for a healthy state of mind within the *Totally^U Framework*, you emerge as an *Interrupter, Awakener,* and *Finisher* in your career. Each unique role assumed gives a fresh and meaningful perspective to bring about insight and enlightenment to your intolerance threshold as you own, reframe, and actualize the stage you identify with. This newfound enlightenment provides the maturity you never previously possessed to deal with work-related psycho-physiological conditions and requirements. It awakens your career possibilities for exponential emotional growth within your place of work.

It is logical from this perspective to develop emotional agility and adaptability that enables you to control your emotional state of mind.

Collectively, the *Totally^U Career Cycle* supports you, a career professional, to endorse and make a more profound connection with your career fallacy. It gives you the best chance to achieve your career aspirations and life goals. No matter how structured and reinforced an emotional experience is in thinking, feeling, responding, relating, and performing, there is no such thing as a safe and guaranteed workplace psychological experience.

While taking care not to frustrate the process, this book cuts right through the chase to the social construct of the professional career state of mind—at least to some extent, one with our choices judicious as our workplace experience. By embracing the truth about our actual state, this book offers a roadmap for your sensory experience. First, it measures the intensity of your state of mind at each stage of the *Career Cycle* to facilitate a shift. Then, it presents you with strategies to motivate you towards or away from the desired change from where you are now in your professional life.

Before we move forward, I have one request, and that is to answer two crucial questions for your benefit:

1. Will you listen to yourself to better unleash your authentic self and release your potential to figure out your professional life?
2. Are you willing to use what you have discovered about yourself to find your balance, hear better what is going on, and start living a contented, happy, and productive professional life?

If you cannot answer "YES" to both questions, you are not ready to start on this particular path to becoming *Totally^U*. It is the moments of heightened awareness, commitment, persistence, resilience, and responsibility that will most significantly influence you to move forward. This will propel the steps towards your growth. Your decision readiness reflects on the emotional state of your current job or career affairs and your motivating energies at each stage of the *Career Cycle—Defeater, Drifter,* or *Achiever*. By the end of this book, I only hope that I will have helped you figure out what's missing.

I look forward to taking you on this journey.

Let's get started.

Chapter 1: The Compass Turns

———

"Life will play you, or you can play life."

On reflection, this statement about life as a game and mastery of strategies to make the best of life was one of the best pieces of advice I was given. In my unconscious state, that sassy blue dress and contoured face were sprinkling bitter lemons on the photographer's behind-the-camera lens. I dimmed the light in the photo studio with the less-than-vibrating energy I charged to my outer world. No one whom I interacted with had asked for this and deserved this energy.

Like a sailor without a compass, I was drifting in my career. On paper, I was successful, yet I was *stuck* with high hopes of achieving a work-life balance. This constantly was at the forefront of my consciousness. While all efforts to create and maintain a healthy balance between completing work and a myriad of personal life responsibilities, my life felt like I was riding the rough tides on seas. Dealing with imposter syndrome, maintaining my personal values, integrity, and caring for both aging parents with demanding health issues was a challenge.

These issues in question were disarrays I needed to cope with while constantly working to create alignment and balance if I wanted to experience a broader quality of life. Moving beyond this default of what was urgent and having any job to keep up with the financial responsibilities to what was important and necessary was not a straightforward task. My body responded to the inner turmoil with a display of emotional self-expression in both my tone and body language. My career was a constant work in progress as I pulled rhythmically, traveling back and forth like the tides of the wave. As a self-actualizing individual, I faced the fear of lost years without realizing that 20 can become 30, then 40, then 50, and then retirement. There were days when I felt I would never "arrive."

I was a ship that was broken at sea, and I felt isolated.

When I reflect on my journey, it was a beautiful challenge, from a life experience embedded with joy, danger, and hardship that provided clarity and the discovery of my life's purpose. Just like life, our career pathway is full of regular tests and trials. When life hits us, we feel most challenged; if we survive, we pass such a test. The thoughts and ideas around tribulation have been around for thousands of years. The patriarch Abraham, from biblical times, had to undergo the ultimate test of offering his son as a sacrifice (Genesis 22:11 KJV) before he realized his life had a purpose. This pedagogy centers on our interaction with learning from lessons along the way. Flourishing in a career takes effort, patience, and time. Assessing our career path is not something that happens overnight.

In crafting this book, I've drawn upon my own experience and that of many others I have met along the way. In common, we rode the career waves and learned how to navigate and evolve while making sense of the corporate world in which we functioned. These individuals were other top performers and high functioning career professionals who were experiencing emotional discomfort in their professional lives. Yet, they eagerly wanted change to experience some type of shift in their careers.

It was comforting to know I was not alone, being employed in an organizational system with a distinct social order so different from my personal rules of conduct and values. The stories shared reminded me of the person I was when life constantly played me, as I repeated self-talks that my childhood career dream would never come alive. But no longer. I now have a career driven by making positive changes. I help by finding solutions for individuals to cope with day-to-day challenges from pressing psychosocial work environments and other societal problems.

Let's face it.

Navigating your life is a job by itself. Job transitions, terrible coworkers, relocation, family issues, unappreciative bosses, work-life balance, and whatever simultaneous roles and responsibilities life throws at you, whether it be titles of mother, father, wife, daughter, son, and team member. The responsibilities that drive your passion in life, coupled with workplace experiences, compete for a position in your life that place you in a daunted mental and emotional state to stay aligned with your career goals.

A standard, typical and played-out scenario sees us finishing a course of study and racking up a large student loan. It leaves us with substantial debt, a qualification we cherish, and yet the job market forces us to pursue a job unrelated to our course of study. All too often, we work a job that only offers a minimum wage to survive. Then, months become years, and we end up with a dwindling aspiration and pursue a job unrelated to our field of study and our career path.

Sometimes, in life, we meet people with whom we have one of the best conversations. And, like the aforementioned photographer, in hindsight, we can foresee the imminent danger of a collision. The photographer framed my psychological coping as a response to a world playing me. In moments like these, we realize that if there were to be a shift as we go through the *Career Cycle*, we would need deep reflection to understand and learn to take control of our emotions and their effects on our careers. This subsequently requires asking the imperative questions "why?" and "how?" Yet these mark only the beginning. The process of awareness does not follow a linear path.

Hence, it is expected that not everyone's growth intensity and duration will be the same. Therefore, it is imperative to understand our personal influence while riding the direction of the waves as we anchor in a place of safety in a career with meaning. Like planning for a wedding, a honeymoon, or graduation, we can identify the stage on our *Career Cycle* in terms of *Achiever, Drifter,* or *Defeater.* Then, we can understand the forces necessary to steer our state of mind as we navigate towards a fulfilling career with a healthy state of mind.

Success Leaves Clues

The profound career fulfillment of incredibly successful people from challenging and diverse backgrounds draws from the power of the same principle as the *Totally^U Framework*—commitment, persistence, resilience, and responsibility. What's interesting is their moment-by-moment emotional reactions to process a balanced life instinctively or purposefully as their careers unfold. Whether these emotions influence specific outcomes depend on choice, endurance, and chance that leads them to find their ultimate success is unknown. Nevertheless, some stories behind the world's most successful people give just a glimpse that you can overcome the odds of passing the resilience test.

Let's take media mogul Oprah Winfrey. After winning the Miss Black Tennessee beauty pageant, she was recruited by WVOL Television to read the news part-time. Her career skyrocketed to host the TV chat show and become the host of her own morning show. *Was this a choice?*

Then, from slicing meat at a deli, billionaire Mark Cuban had various jobs; he successfully created and sold his first computer consulting company—Micro Solutions. He later sold it to CompuServe—then a subsidiary of the multi-national American tax preparation company—H&R Block. *Was this by chance?*

Cesar R. Hernandez started his career working with youths as a community organizer after being arrested six times on criminal charges and later became a leader in the business community. His ambition was persistent and a catalyst for change and he served as an example. He now advises some of the world's brightest minds. *Was this because of endurance?*

The journey to our destined career within the stages of this *Cycle* is not set in stone. This is why constant self-reflection and the improvement of our thoughts within the *Career Cycle* are unique to each of us. Although our work environments may be quite different, as career professionals, we all want clarity to know our purpose and align it with our career, family, and spirituality. The *Career Cycle* is ever-evolving, and so are our states of mind. Some may be still adrift. What we want and get at the end of the day can be far apart. What excites today may not excite next year, and as career purpose shifts, many walk around dazed. Perhaps confused, stuck, and left reeling in a fight-or-flight mode from the unpleasantness and intolerance of their current stage. Alternately, they may not even know what their purpose is. Others may remain wrapped up in their self-identity, have been egotistical, and are unaware they are going through a cycle.

By clarifying our thoughts, we will have proven that we are indeed captains of our ship, and we can flourish in our intended careers. We will remain a verb as we ride low tides and high tides to become our best. To achieve a successful career, we need to be adaptable to break away from the undesired stage of our current reality. Once identified, possibilities are awakened to an ideal career we yearn for and want in the future.

My *Career Cycle* was a fascinating process, having fallen within the *Achiever*, the *Drifter*, and the *Defeater* stage of the *Career Cycle* throughout my career. However, once I got honest about my facts and feelings, the journey was magical. Internal "conflicts" of feeling overwhelmed, disoriented, stuck, frustrated, and in a panic, my professional career story changed. The words of the photographer and my personal degrees of validity led to an embodied shift. These were enough to motivate a change within me.

Chapter 2: Paving the Way

———

Our backgrounds may differ, yet many of us still yearn for the same thing—we seek a personal balance of a "career" in a state of flow with commitment, persistence, resilience, and responsibility. A career that allows us to feel connected within the universe and experience a profound sense of belonging in spirituality, family, and work.

So far, your previous choices and actions were a guide to influence your current thoughts and actions and ignite your desires to gain or regain optimal functioning within your career. Now, as you read about the components of the *Totally^U Framework* and each stage of the *Career Cycle*, you will become more cognizant of some unanswered questions or reminiscence of the career you once had.

The Career Cycle

The moment you start to work, you enter what I refer to as a recurring *Career Cycle*. This conceptual *Career Cycle* is divided into three parts, with no section directly opposite another. The *Career Cycle* is not intended to define you professionally, and my approach and my ethos are one of *empowerment* in all areas of your life. I am not the person to judge or place labels on anyone, and as we move forward, I aim not to label an individual as a winner, loser, success, failure, right or wrong. From professional and personal experience, I know this type of labeling limits both an intellectual and a spiritual level of growth.

Figure 1: Totally^U Career Cycle

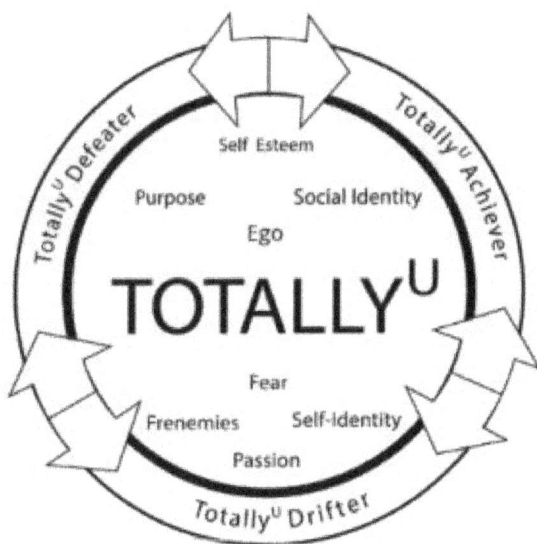

THE *Career Cycle* demonstrates multiple factors contributing to where you might find yourself within the cycle and bring this to life. I identify three stages—*Drifter, Achiever,* and *Defeater.* These stages are part of the recurring cycle you may pass through as your career thrives or wanes. It is important to note the stages are not sequential steps to move from one stage of the cycle to another. You can make shifts unilaterally.

The stages describe and explore your spontaneous and deliberate responses and attitudes towards your current realities and your state of mind. They provide clues between contentment and discontentment of your work situations at any stage you are in. All three stages, the *Drifter*, the *Achiever*, and the *Defeater*, are different, yet the emotional responses to triggers at work can all add up when they emerge at the surface. By considering the stage you may currently perform at can reveal whether you are: (i) successful in your career, (ii) just getting by, or (iii) have given up.

Along your journey within the *Career Cycle*, your current realities provide a base from which to explore where your life is now, compared to where you ideally would like to be. This can be likened to the visual representation and the Buddhist concept of the "Wheel of Life." A Buddhist visual depiction of the endless rotation as a cycle of our existence— "death," "rebirth," and "suffering."

Using the Wheel of Life as a conceptual representation, your spur-of-the-moment and thoughtful responses and attitudes towards emotional triggers may lead to the actualization of your career dream or the eventual death of your career, as you suffer through conflicts as you experience a rebirth that moves you closer to the desired stage.

There are positive and negative aspects to each stage. Understanding the set characteristics to follow of an *Achiever, Drifter,* and *Defeater* stage can significantly raise your lid to welcome a shift for finding an ideal reality. As you move through these stages, you are guided away from a current stage and towards a more desired one to optimize your experience in each one, rather than succumb to its challenges. I am a mediator between *Drifter, Defeater*, and *Achiever* in sound logic, especially epistemology.

Career Burners

Within the *Career Cycle*, you operate with competing forces affecting your emotional state for transition throughout the cycle from one stage to another. You function as a variant of your personal truth, reflecting all that is open, concealed, and yet to be discovered. The emphasis of each interpersonal attribute within the *Career Cycle* is what I refer to as your burners—Self-identity with reflections of Social Identity, Ego and Self Esteem, Passion and Purpose, and Career and Vocation. Each burner symbolizes one major area of your life, and they operate the same on each of the three stages of the cycle.

We learn, we live, and we love as our burners conflict, representing reality and varnished truth. For example, the Ego reflects self-esteem, and passion and purpose can become entangled. Your burners are the ultimate flaw that causes suffering, guilt, shame, emotional pain, and satisfactoriness throughout the different stages of the cycle. In line with the foundations and premise of Buddhist teachings of the Wheel of Life, your personal attributes represent "poison." They unveil a web of less conscious psychological interrelated issues that may shine a light on familiar old problems. These are the realities that help you either evolve or repeat negative emotions that disrupt your career state of flow.

Noticing any conflict of these interpersonal attributes will determine how quickly you transition from a less desired to a more desired stage within the *Career Cycle* and how you remain present in this stage. If not managed to your advantage, interpersonal attributes adversely impact your encounters as a *Defeater, Drifter*, or an *Achiever*. They may be a key cause of the psychological challenges and adverse unconscious temporal behavioral patterns. If mismanaged, they become rooted in what leads to the creation of delusion, confusion, and greed aversion. On the other hand, if managed well, they provide clarity, confidence, and contentment.

The "U" Concept

———

A t the center of the *Career Cycle* is *"U"* as a career professional. The *U* embraces your interpersonal attributes to gain clarity at each stage of the cycle. As such, job titles are irrelevant. Collectively, over time, the *U* concept creates a pattern of behavior that determines one's energy, consciousness, and state of mind to fall within the *Achiever, Drifter*, and *Defeater* stage. *U* becomes an exponential function as you coagulate a practical plan for your psychological growth that preserves and enhances your career professional's identity. You become more aware of your burners and emotional state and begin to take control to identify the stage you find yourself within—*Totally^{U}Achiever, Totally^U Drifter,* or a *Totally^U Defeater.* You then create emotional balance to unfold your unlimited potential within your work environment. The "U" embraces defying efforts for self-change, to move away from one stage and towards your desired stage within the *Totally^{U}Career Cycle.*

The Totally^U Framework

Knowledge is power. Knowledge is not defined by statistics or education level. Knowledge leads to awareness in identifying basic patterns, which leads to our newfound awareness's actions, giving us the energy and propulsion for learning and implementation. At this point, education becomes knowledge, and knowledge can come from anywhere. We are then presented with choices to fulfill our desires or interests as we gain more courage to compromise and state what we want.

The *Totally^{U}Framework* embraces the connectedness to spirituality, family, and work that develops certainty and confidence, and we become more likely to learn. To develop clarity for the connectedness of spirituality, family, and work, we take on self-supporting roles of an *Interrupter, Awakener*, and *Finisher*. The assumed roles give a fresh perspective of the intolerance threshold to excitedly bring about meaningful change as we own, reframe, and actualize the stage we identify with. As we begin, we develop a clear state of mind. *The Totally^U Framework* provides newfound enlightenment—one that offers the insight and skills to work effectively with career-related psychological experiences. An awakened knowledge aimed at aligning core values for the emotional balance needed for exponential emotional growth within our careers.

From observations, encounters, and personal experience, I conclude the journey is more important than any formal education. However, the most substantial level you can start is not identifying yourself with a stage. Introspective and foundational work done with clients who were vulnerable in their careers facilitated the learning to develop strategies for a change within the *Totally*^{U} *Framework*. From here on, everything is *Totally* *"U."* You are "in control," as you have a reflective understanding of what needs to change and where you are within the cycle—*Achiever, Drifter*, or *Defeater.*

You are about to discover uncomfortable truths as you act and create a blend of your passion, ego, identity, and purpose so that together, the fundamentals of these personal and interpersonal attributes merge for you to harness the power of self-knowledge and propel your career.

Chapter 3: A Career State of Mind

———

We socially share our emotions and conscious reasoning of our career path during our career journey and across disciplines. Often, the stories shared are emotional synchrony of career ideals intertwining with our current career successes. One of chance, choice, or endurance. We paint some of these in our commitment to family, faith, community, and behavioral attitudes. These clashing commitments and unconscious induction of our emotional states place us within the $Totally^U$ Career Cycle. We can quickly become accustomed to just getting by and not keeping our career options open.

Like many, I struggled to find idealism versus realism in an age of economic globalization. An array of work-related issues affected me: downsizing, resizing, restructuring, artificial intelligence that depleted job skills, and organizational systems presented themselves differently in the real world. I realized this personally and by working with others. Conversations and observations shared with me over the years pointed to the fact that this was a common occurrence.

The best place to balance this conversation of a mental construct and an actual view of the situation was through a poll on LinkedIn. I posed the following question:

Q: Have you found that companies show inconsistencies and have shortcomings in their business style of operations after being hired?

Six hundred respondents made their position clear.

The results?

A: Over ninety percent stated "Yes!"

To make sense of everything further, discovery sessions with my clients revealed it was not about adjusting resumes to match job description advertisements. Instead, there was something profound about finding employment and staying employed. Once I realized this, it changed everything.

After dedicating years to studying and progressing through education levels, the reality of work-life was a slap in the face. Advanced education was not a guarantee for better pay. We would surmise that education was a way to advance on the social-economic ladder. This is the story we are 'sold,' but after a while, we are conscious of what is happening, becoming so immersed in the environment with little control. No wonder many career professionals operate on autopilot—with no rhythm or flow.

If you can relate to the above, make no mistake to think you are the only one going through, or have gone through this. It may comfort you to know that I fell into all three stages at some point in my life—the *Achiever*, *Drifter*, and *Defeater*.

The perpetual *Career Cycle* affects your work performance and socializing with peers. Coupled with your subjective internal forces, it poses a severe psychological liability. It will have you continuously checking with your mind to find some connection between past desires and your current reality. Like myself, the unearned reality of my own career experiences did not meet my expectations. I tied up my past, present, and future in priorities, values, and purpose, like a kind of multidimensional time warp.

Preconceived reality brought even more risks and challenges to my state of mind. As a furiously curious person, this disruption tapped into my conscious mind, leading me to ask questions of myself: Where was my path? How could I pave the way for purposes and meanings in my career journey? My only conclusion then; I was not merely confused but lost.

In this state of confusion and loss, I became misguided and in denial of the information about my shortcomings. I did not know what the hell I was doing. Every aspect of my life lost frequency. I did not align my mind, body, feelings, and thoughts with my whole being. My body responded to the disruptions through pain and internal conflict that eventually led to unemployment and workplace difficulties with my superiors. I was dragged through a maze continuously flushed and sullen with anger, irritability, and exasperation. As I was indignant, it manifested itself in a demonstrative fashion. As my directions changed, healing started with hard conversations started by a total stranger that would have given my life story a great end.

We are all given a script that unconsciously comes with an attached status quo and big promises from the get-go in childhood. Even if your career journey does not provide a smooth, linear experience, the ideal job feels similar to a lucid dream. Go to school, get good grades, land a great job, and move up the corporate ladder, and by society's definition, you become successful. Without realizing it, this script gets reinforced through the years. No one taught you to unlearn the script that no longer serves you. As you become adults like an unwelcomed opportunity, reality sinks in. You need to do more, earn more, and be of significance! Even more, you have an urge to fit in. As you scan your environment for hyperarousal states, you are more conscious of your work environment.

At this personal level, your current state's self-awareness comes from conversations with the various parts of yourself that cause you to lose your focus and balance. At this point, you know one thing for sure:

childhood daydreaming stops being fun. Indeed, your career journey contains much more than what you may have bargained for. You come to terms with reality and begin seeing every job and work situation for exactly what it is. Viewing your career as a choice, chance or endurance.

The positive experiences you have at each stage will promote meaningfulness and create greater opportunities for transition between stages. The transition to crossing over from one stage to another doesn't get easier. As prosaic as it sounds, change often happens when you become motivated to change by some painful, life-altering external forces—for example, personal losses and unemployment. Discovering yourself at each stage takes a lot of effort. It requires you to block the unconscious noise of discrediting yourself with common questions such as "Why is this other person progressing, and I am not?" or "When did I become a loser?"

With a glimpse of your reality and a more profound sense of the stage you are in, you can interpret the wrong and right turns of who you are as a professional and whether or not you are standing on still water. With time, you start to listen and attach to the sound of the waves you want to hear. Then, with each move of the sea, you get stronger, and you start dancing to the right rhythm of the waves.

Chapter 4: Totally^U Prejudices

—————

Whenever I introduce the *Totally^U* concept and ask career professionals where they fall within the *Framework*, their reactions are mixed with some individuals not knowing where to place themselves. Not knowing is understandable. As humans, we have a solid desire to be captain of our lives and control over our career outcomes—"*I know what I want, I can do it by myself*" is the most significant prejudice. It is easiest to understand, especially with our years of experience and education, to support this. However, the fact remains that many other influences can take control of the stage we find ourselves in.

A *Totally^U Achiever*, *Totally^U Drifter*, and a *Totally^U Defeater* stage manifest differently in everyone within the *Career Cycle*. It is not a one-size-fits-all. Neither is it a gradual progression through one stage nor between one extreme and another. Being within the *Totally^U Drifter* stage does not require moving through the *Totally^U Defeater* stage to the *Totally^U Achiever* stage. To avoid the confusion and distortion about the *Totally^U Defeater, Totally^U Drifter*, and a *Totally^U Achiever* stage is not to be considered in one or the other exclusively. To reiterate, neither stage is entirely in charge of our conduct or behavior. However, the intensity of affective emotions in each stage is captured on the level of the emotional intensity as a responsive behavior over some time.

Individuals within the *Achiever, Drifter*, and *Defeater* stage do not remain at the same stage throughout their careers. It is possible to continuously travel along the path of choice, endurance, and change state of mind in each stage. Similarly, you may go through the stages a few times. At any one of the stages, you are either functioning by chance and barely holding on, or going anywhere the winds blow, you go. You have checked out from your career dreams.

On the other hand, you may be mindful of the stage, accept the implication of the practical evaluation, and endure your current situation as satisfaction. Alternatively, you can exercise the choices with tight control of your emotions and the environment's forces to live out your career dreams. As such, you only need little support to shift from one stage to another.

The stops at each stage and between the extremes of choice, endurance, and chance unfold a story that catalyzes deeper self-awareness and an entry point to experience every moment of your self-discovery journey. To act or not. As you sail through on the rhythm of the *Career Cycle*, you will come to terms with what causes a "thorn in your flesh," as Paul the Apostle describes in his account of annoyance in his life (2 Corinthians 12:7-10 KJV). This revelation will drive you to investigate further to find your career compass or land you in a place of denial.

Those who survive from the position of a *Totally^U Drifter* and a *Totally^U Defeater* or maintain a *Totally^U Achiever* stage become intentional. Once located accurately within the *Totally^U Career Cycle*, they are bold and brave enough to gain liberating insight and no longer let adversity define their career journey moving forward.

Knowing your position is your first stage of renouncing self-conscious emotion and elicitation that mediates self-enhancement.

Taking Ownership

———

Time waits for no one. Becoming real captains and controlling your own ship's sails require placing hands on the helm for control. It is much easier to work with things in your field of awareness rather than having them unconsciously sabotage your career. When you leave things in the dark regarding your career, they start to affect your life in ways you are not even aware of, preventing you from growing professionally. Informed decisions are better than uninformed ones. Once collectively identified, the elements of a *Totally^U Defeater*, *Totally^U Achiever*, and *Totally^U Drifter* can change those not aligned with your core values to create a more enabling and fulfilling work experience. That is when knowledge becomes power.

As a career professional, you need to make sense of the world you live in beyond your externals of job titles within an organization. All you have now is yourself to consult with as you search for answers that haven't yet formed. Unprepared and overwhelmed from never having the ability to filter what is important and what isn't, can make you feel like you walk around with decision fatigue as you try to adjust to your career. This emphasizes further the need to identify the career stage where you are at. Otherwise, you risk turning into someone who lives their life rooted without conscious thought and in a robotic existence. Unfortunately, you experience your career mindlessly, never to see yourself beyond how you currently exist.

Your adjustment styles drive your correspondence of satisfaction with your work environment or a clash of harmony at work. First, an adjustment style depends on your willingness to change your work environment to reduce the current level of dissatisfaction. And this depends mainly on your flexibility and adaptability to move from or *toward* your desired stage. Second, it is by changing your narrative and the actions taken to alleviate the dissatisfaction experienced in the workplace. How well you can continue to tolerate this dissatisfaction shows your mastery of the *Totally^U Framework*.

Adjusting your behavior before either giving up or leaving your work situation altogether requires commitment, persistence, resilience, and responsibility. Changing yourself means expanding your awareness and increasing your emotional intelligence and psychological flexibility. A sustainable, harmonious professional career life or stage shift is possible by changing job and/or changes in the work environment requirements. This is what organizational psychologists call a person-environment factor.

The Theory of Work Adjustment (TWA) clarifies career professionals' relationship with their work environment. They mutually influence each other in a few ways. First, a career professional has requirements that can be satisfied by the work environment and vice versa. Second, they both have capacities to meet the work environment requirements. When both parties in this relationship are happy, no change happens. However, if one or both parties become dissatisfied, an adjustment must occur.

Sadly, our work environment can be toxic, and in such cases, the attempt to adjust does not happen easily. Here, a career professional must change too much by sacrificing essential needs. As a result, work motivation extends from satisfaction to dissatisfaction. Remember, your personal adjustment styles drive your willingness to tolerate any career progress. This means changing your emotions, needs, and possibly your skills.

Finding the alignment of your own career burners in your current stage means sitting with yourself for a while to unravel the most profound emotions. Hence, I cannot stress this enough, you must recognize the stage you are in. The action taken to clear the roadblocks will largely depend on what it threatens with attached psychological suffering in your career and personal life. Only with a broader and more goal-oriented perspective can you capture career-depleting habits. Exponential leaps and infinite possibilities are authoritative, taking small steps for the desired outcome. This is the optimum *Totally*^{U}.

Every stage of the cycle has unique challenges that you'll need to face. Each of us has our own life sensitivities that collide with careers. We all know that life is unpredictable. A strong wind can blow and throw you off course, even when you have achieved career success. Those career professionals who survive do so because they become intentional about their hidden drivers to figure out new and original ways of thinking, feeling, and behaving.

A glimpse of where you are right now is an indispensable requisite for a career rebirth. Change is an inevitable part of your career across your lifespan. If you want to prosper and experience a state of abundance and prosperity in your profession, you must adapt to the constant state of flux that turns within the *Totally*^{U} *Career Cycle*.

Chapter 5: The Totally^U Defeaters

———

Nothing could have prepared me for what I was about to encounter as I entered the room to conduct an intake assessment for an adult family home resident. I wasn't prepared for a powerful, repulsive smell that emanated from the apartment. A strong sour smell of food and alcohol reminded me of days-old, fermented tomato sauce. Gerry, a mid-career professional, sat in the gastric secretions and urine surrounded by quarts of empty whiskey bottles. When we met, Gerry's conversations about his past work environment triggered explicit emotions about his job. Mighty ones. It motivated him to choose a longer-term reactive response. He'd made an expensive choice. To Gerry, "a whiskey bottle held hope." He'd succumbed to alcohol over a career as a high-paid C-Suite Executive.

There is a proverb that states if you want to know the truth, speak to a drunk person. Sitting with Gerry, he emphasized he was the first in his family to go to college and to work his way up the career ladder. He lamented that the stressors of work-life balance landed him drunk on most days, his work performance fell, and of course, they fired him. The demands of his job and family were lessons Gerry tried to make sense of, alongside everything else around him. Gerry wondered how he got into this predicament, and a conversation emerged as he rationalized his divorce from his wife of thirty years. He was upset with everything and everyone.

As Gerry cast judgment on his career, he showed little compassion for who he was as a person long before he was given titles or labels. Without his knowledge or control, Gerry became dragged down by a state of discontentment and what he saw in those moments is what he chose. Such conditions were enough to designate his need to surrender and signalled his place within the $Totally^U$ Defeater stage in his work situation.

A typical person within the $Totally^U$ Defeater stage will compare themselves to others or even a former version of themselves. As I became more acquainted with Gerry, his story never changed as he reminisced. His past successful career talks and the sensory experience was a well-delivered speech. As he spoke, I could see his sense of validation, saying, "*I was once important.*" With different variations of his talk, he amplified his career challenges and sank himself deeper into the center of his mental world, thinking the entire universe conspired against him. Gerry ended up trapping himself in trying to escape a vicious $Totally^U$ Defeater stage and go searching for one of his friends—Mr. Vodka or Mr. Hennessey.

Career professionals experiencing the $Totally^U$ Defeater stage try to succeed with no progress. Despite being given the best chance to achieve their career aspirations and life goals, discontentment sets in. *Defeaters* work with one equation and one equation only, and this is a mismatch of the past tense of what was and the future tense of how it should be.

Those within the *TotallyU Defeaters* stage start from wandering thoughts early. These thoughts patterns form a guide for making excuses to paint attitudes towards work. As their job pulls them in many directions, the focus goes where energy flows. Valuation-based choices cause them to flee from the work environment and the world that may seem fake.

Finding a place within the *Totally^U Defeater* stage, career professionals are mindlessly on automation. They are at the total mercy of incoming stimuli or influences that send them sailing out of their careers. Coupled with a hostile underlying work environment, such as micromanagement, they are predisposed to repetitive negative thought processes that their effort is worth nothing. As their emotional experiences get "hot," their thoughts are not innovative nor revolutionary. The handling of emotional pain and psychological hurts emphasized by anguish, despair, and anxiety is part of the experience of individuals within the *Defeater* stage.

The flight or fight mode is in a constant high alert for an emerging *Totally^U Defeater*. The thought of being defeated motivates them to aggress, try to escape the pain, or sometimes, cause them to freeze. These emotional experiences help to make a prominent shift to the *Defeater* stage. I believe there is nothing wrong with being within the *Defeater* stage if we rise to the point of genuine growth. The pervasive characteristic of being within the *Defeater* stage of the *Totally^U Career Cycle* is that you want to avoid. Thoughts at this stage are competing between evidence of truth and current reality.

The vigilant emotions you are trying to prevent cause more damage and require greater psychological skills for flexibility of adaptation. Retrieving, recalling, and reconstructing information is a fundamental precursor to too much human thinking, decision making, and action. Never confuse a career defeat with a *final* career defeat, as they are poles apart. The lesson here is not to let your career define who you are as a person. Your social identity is very much different from self-identification. Suppose you face these roadblocks and hurdles while within the *Defeate*r stage; use them as a motivation to clean up your emotions and move on.

The opportunity to secure ourselves against defeat then lies in our own hands. More power to you if you are in a *Defeater* stage and you can withstand the storm, and your soul can endure your situation's conditions without losing your peace.

Early Defeat

———

My first actual dose of internal challenges occurred at the end of two-years-of age. I had trouble imitating sounds. My action over vocalizations to communicate did not produce words. I wanted to speak with other children, but I could not even if I tried. The same holds true when I found myself within the *Totally^U Defeater* stage: wishing to be in another stage of success to match my education, yet hard work would not get me there.

My own sensitivities did not differ from Albert Einstein, who also had a language development delay. I failed to speak until I was seven years of age with no medical diagnosis. I was considered "dumb" and unable to communicate with my peers, teachers, and educators. I was held back in kindergarten until I was seven. Each year, teacher after teacher drew the same conclusion. I would never speak. For years, my babbles remained even though I understood verbal requests. I used gestures and pointing to communicate my immediate needs.

A Dad was always going to be a true protector with his unexpressed love and care. Following a harsh punishment from one of my teachers to justify my true belief of having a speech disability, my father hauled me to another school. Unimpressed, he insisted I should be among other children my age and grade level. He no longer accepted anything less. To Daddy, his daughter could hear, which was enough for him. He knew I was not cognitively impaired—it took me no longer to respond to stimuli than others. He knew his paternal intellectual obligations would limit the adverse impact of my experiences. His confidence and belief undoubtedly fostered some self-belief in me, diluting the damaging impact of school.

My personal defeat was a moral discourse from those around me that became a fact in this limiting world. The delayed speech and its psychological effects subtly filtered into my adulthood. The not-so-satisfying emotional experiences lay dormant only to appear later in life and present themselves as imposter syndrome, low confidence, and lack of self-esteem. For years I held the belief that— *"I have achieved in my careers through luck and chance rather than talent or skill."*

However, I was a ship not built to stay in a harbor. I forged and highlighted compelling lessons by changing the narrative of my not speaking, not doubting my abilities and achievements, and childhood experiences. So, without being bothered, I adopted the knowledge that I was not "dumb," and I overcame the most limiting beliefs that had developed in my young brain. This was tough, especially given that the first five years of a child's learning is the most critical period to their overall life trajectory. The brain learns faster than at any other time as a two-year-old and within the first 1000 days of life.

In summary, individuals within the *Totally^U Defeaters* stage try to make sense of their situation, which can be pointless and meaningless. They constantly reflect if they will survive in it—much less thrive. To justify their belief and avoid the experiences of emptiness, they are drawn towards co-dependencies of destructive habits at their own expense. This is the type of emotion you try to avoid when wanting to move to a more desired stage. They yearn to stop the real world and safely navigate back to their childhood career dream. They eventually succumb to hopelessness and despondency, and dependency between actuality and reality.

This is the type of emotion if used constructively, defeat can be a valuable teacher. Learning is not a defeat. You see, the pebbles you may have collected while wobbling in your defeat can be gold if you remain hungry for learning, sharing, and growing. Within my neurological threshold, listening became my strength. I cultivated humility and reverence for listening to other people who seek a fulfilled career and a life of purpose.

Chapter 6: The Totally^U Drifters

The day Susan told me she snapped at one of her juvenile clients, she asked me to visit her office. Between our conversations and her work, she recorded minute-by-minute accounts of every action. At her level of seniority and career spanning twenty-two years, she explained she was asked to literally document her every action each working day. She was exasperated and expressed her frustration towards clients and those leading her. She could not understand the course of her career development and the childhood dream career she had. She wanted to serve people as a Nurse.

In the early days, she had little choice but to accept her career because it allowed her the flexibility to raise her three boys. Her shift ended at 3 pm—just in time to pick up her children from school. But once her children were finished with college, her circumstances changed the compass for the direction of her ship. The work environment she found herself in made her feel defeated. She continually bore the injustice of an inadequate reward and mental suffering imposed by micromanagement. Quietly she drifted.

Susan had mentioned her pay grade to management and, in addition, had discussed her need to be with her aging parent. Each time, management dismissed her. Then, employing a higher paid "part-time" labor with lower skills, who Susan had to train, cut her deeply. Finally, the anchor for Susan's ship broke. Instead of the Old Testament principle of a reciprocal measure of justice, an "eye for an eye" (Exodus

21:23-27 KJV) retribution influenced a career of defeat, Susan adjusted her behavior. She resigned.

Individuals within the *Totally^U Drifters* stage do not sail in a straight line. Instead, they aimlessly cruise through a life of being employed. *Drifters* spend most of their time flirting with career transition ideas. Career professionals in this stage go to school, get a job, switch jobs, find a spouse, move from house to house, place to place, and eventually retire. They flow along the path of chance and endurance, happy to have a job. They comfortably think their career is what it is, and there is nothing they can do about it. They boldly balance their feelings of fear by playing it safe or in a quiet way, along with the disappointment, embarrassment, loss, change, and the truth of their career's motivation.

Drifter's relationships, especially with people, are riddled with conditions and expectations for helping them change their current stage as they travel a timeless journey along the *Totally^U Career Cycle*. They can appear calm and successful in public yet become a failure in private. Their state of mind resonates with Paul Williams's quote, "It is the not-knowingness of things as they truly are, or of oneself as one really is."

Like Gerry, some people within the *Defeater Stage* go with the flow and drift away into having no career and living a life of regret. Others, such as Susan, continuously strain toward consciousness, maintain a state of repression, and become confronted by their own despair, and this becomes a learning moment. Learning is not losing, and if you learn from being defeated, you haven't really lost.

Defeat can be a valuable teacher. Some people learn the wrong lessons, like Gerry, who shrank further into the disappearance. However, sometimes it can be constructive. The day Susan's husband of thirty-two years called to thank me for sending his wife back home,

I knew Susan's boat had docked safely to another stage within the *Totally^U Career Cycle.*

Subtly, misconception and ignorance about reality lead to a career professional within the *Drifter Stage* grasping and clinging to repeated rebirths rather than evolving. They wandered like the Israelites in the wilderness in a desert region for forty years, unable to find a way to an inhabited city (Psalm 107:40 KJV). Sometimes powerless to shape their career destiny. It is easy for them to become cynical, fatalistic, and bitter, especially when dejection, anxiety, despair, and helplessness emerge just thinking about work on a Sunday night. The grueling thought and reluctance of walking through the office doors on a Monday are almost too much to bear.

Professionals within the *Totally^U Drifters* stage operate on a journey of co-sensing and presencing, as described and illustrated at the organizational level by Otto Scharmer, Organizational Psychologist. This is comparable and applicable to the *Totally^U Framework* at the individual level. These two processes are dynamic as they connect a future career reality with the reality that individuals within the *Totally^U Drifter Stage* currently face.

On the one hand, it highlights the emerging reality that wants to happen around them and within them. Their co-sensing carries with it present thoughts, constant observation, and listening with their mind and heart wide open to justify within themselves why a change in a stage is necessary. One thought-provoking question I posed to Susan—*What would happen should she leave her job, and what would not happen if she were to stay?* This question provided an insight into why the transition was necessary and how reclaiming an amazing career as a Nurse would impact her professional and personal life.

The presencing process signifies our heightened state of attention, psychological flexibility, and the psychological shifts in our thoughts, language, and patterns of behavior. It is being present in the moment of what we feel and sense. An exciting new way of thinking emerges as we create new neural pathways from outside of our usual awareness and thinking. Connecting with the self, reflecting on the decision-making process, self-management, and mindfulness allows the $Totally^U$ Drifters to shift the inner place from which they function.

Job satisfaction drives behavior for the career professional within the $Totally^U$ Drifter stage. One indicator of work adjustment anchored on Dawis & Lofquist (1984) is the Person-environment Correspondence Theory on individual differences in traditional vocational behavior—satisfactoriness. A $Totally^U$ Drifter's needs are reinforced by their work environment, leading to their stay time within the job. An extreme response to dissatisfaction is founded on intensity, pattern, and duration. Hence, the spectrum state of mind of an individual's current reality will influence the extremes of these variables. A $Totally^U$ Drifter may or may not be happy depending on their environment and how they react and adapt. Suppose we view the career professional as symmetrical to their environment. In that case, the goal is to have jobs that reflect the individuals' needs, values, abilities that align and support an emotional state. However, moving out of this stage can become asymmetrical when both response requirements and reinforcement capabilities are not met.

A $Totally^U$ Drifter career professional is in a state of chance, can go through life with no other purpose than collecting a paycheck. Yet, there is an anchored belief that their career lacks rhyme or reason with their thoughts. For the $Totally^U$ Drifters, in a state of mind of endurance, every day on the job is just like a wave, every moment is a tide, and there is little they feel they can do once the weather changes course. This is especially the case when an organization remains stuck in institutionalized thinking. Without support from their work environment, individuals make it their choice to stay within the *Totally*^{U} *Drifter* stage. Or they can shield themselves when needed, most especially when protection is not available elsewhere in the working environment. Strong support from their team or managers is needed for *Totally*^{U} *Drifters*, as change occurs at an organizational level.

Individuals within the *Totally*^{U} *Drifters* stage can be caught in the current like the ocean's force and the wind direction. Waiting to crash into the rocks and drift further to sea. One example is when I had a heavy workload. I had inadequate effort-reward imbalance, poor management, unclear expectations of work, and increasingly heightened responsibilities. These factors are stressors and known precursors to mental and physical ill-health, and alongside my presumed psychological flexibility, can lead to physical health deterioration. Yet being within the *Totally*^{U} *Drifter stage*, my emerging emotions to get to my desired stage helped protect me from burnout and other negative consequences, including disliking myself.

Titles and a considerable salary were not alluring. Personal values are important to me; they motivate and guide my behavior to avoid a lack of work-life balance. However, a heavy dose of reality led me to choose that I would neither be riding in an ambulance nor a hearse with a collision of personal values versus organizational expectations. Persons *drifting* operate from the future as they wait to emerge to another stage. All I could think was that there was more to work than this. I eventually resigned.

Presencing and co-sensing played their part.

Being within the *TotallyU Drifters* stage, co-sensing and the presencing processes are subjective and not linear. Life is easier to live in the moment and becomes the default strategy. It is typical for individuals on this stage to place their career foes in the addiction's pocket family, an idea, or another human being. Take Marsha, a former coworker and single mother. She was constantly sipping from her coffee cup, and the assumption, like many others, was that Marsha was reliant on caffeine. So, imagine the surprise when it came to light during one lunch trip to the local grocery store that her coffee indulgence was Smirnoff Vodka. She used this to relieve her endurance state of mind and function peacefully with compassion to clients on the phone. It was a workday completed to her utmost satisfaction; her personal way of dealing with being within the *Totally^U Drifter* stage.

Once a career professional within the *TotallyU Drifters* stage accepts a dejection, it can be an experience in random order, wildly jumping backward with repeat processes as they are caught in the moment. When that shift happens, they begin to operate from a space they believe wants to emerge. With a sense of growth and accomplishment, setting meaningful goals and emotional agility guards against unfairness, disrespect, and the mismatch between workplace and personal values that eradicate conflicting emotions. Engagements in empathy walk to imagine another person who is drifting and generative creativity for new patterns of behavior act as internal representations for the exponential growth of career possibilities beyond a *Totally^U Drifter* stage.

Within the *Totally^U Drifter* stage, there is a high dependence on your emotional state and your cognitive commitment to encourage progression from the *Totally^U Drifter* stage to a more desired alternative. However, I have found that individuals as a *Totally^U Drifter* can enhance their ability to move forward by gaining insight into the true nature of their personal reality and moving beyond their current state. However, it is easier said than done as they make their next stop at either the *Defeater* or A*chiever* stage.

Chapter 7: TheTotally^U Achievers

Troy can clearly remember the day the local firefighters came to his Pre-K school when he was five. From the big red fire truck to the giant ladders, with lights flashing and the loud siren blaring, the firefighters appeared larger than life. Wearing bulky coats and pants made them look extra-large and lifelike superheroes. It was the most extraordinary performance he had ever seen. He gleefully watched these marvelous superheroes disembark the fire truck like Batman, visiting him in his Batmobile. Without a doubt, this cast confirmation in his mind that he wanted to be one of those firefighters. His vision of wearing an authentic firefighter uniform made him ecstatic.

For Troy, there was no other career choice. He had a career dream and was fully committed to this critical life event. Even at the tender age of five, his "Why?" might not have been crystal clear back then. However, he certainly understood the importance of a firefighter and the towering responsibility when he entered the *Totally^U Career Cycle*.

When I met Troy, he'd shared his journey and beamed in delight. He'd followed his north star and the direction that was right for him. It was no longer a figment of his imagination at twenty-three years old. With Paramedic School finished, he applied for a city job and was eager to pursue his childhood dream career. Troy encapsulates the perfect career hero and stands as a role model as he achieves his vision. He is the ideal career professional within the *Totally^U Achiever* stage.

Individuals within the *Totally^U Achievers* stage pick up the right signals without adjusting their radar antennas. They detect all aspects throughout their life–career, marriages, and friendships. They are the ones within an organization who consistently meet and exceed performance goals and expectations. While these individuals are not necessarily gifted, no matter their challenges, they seem to rise to the top of the corporate ladder as they journey along the way in their careers. They just burst into everything and travel through life with an incredible sense of direction. They know their "whys," and they perfect their pitch.

In his book Skin in the Game, Nassim Nicholas Taleb, a former Options Trader, best explains how career professionals within the *Totally^U Achievers* stage get to where they are. "What you do is the purest definition of your value system."

Likewise, in his influential book, *Start with Why* Simon Sinek states, "Your actions demonstrate what you believe." These statements validate values and goals are coherent within the *Totally^U Achievers* stage.

Totally^U Achiever stage professionals possess strong perceptual skills which guide them in their careers, home life, and relationships. They may even have careers not associated with popularity, power or possessions, or the societal definition of success, but their traits define them. When we see individuals like this and identify the critical characteristics, we'd agreeably conclude they are grounded. They may have affluent friends and are driven to match their experiences, often making them feel they are within the *Totally^U Drifter* and *Totally^U Defeater* stage. With each comes its own psychological impact. of successful career professionals, *Totally^U Achiever* stage professionals own their happiness within their job. They, at times, will enjoy a career that merges harmoniously with their purpose.

While some people find their focus early in life, the truth is that *Totally^U Achievers* stage professionals are made and not born. Being within the *Totally^U Achiever's* stage is a choice state of mind. It is not limited to only those with remarkable social and emotional intelligence. Years of consistently mastering and managing their emotional state in times of challenge set them apart. Elon Musk is a typical *Achiever*. Musk brought incredible focus and passion to the things that interested him. He decided his goals and then focused his actions and intensity on continuing within the *Totally^U Achiever* stage for his future quest. He is outstanding at everything he tries, and Tesla, SpaceX, Zip2, and PayPal are just a few of the companies he has been behind.

Like Troy, Musk's trajectory was a choice he made early in life. At twelve years old, abstract thinking, problem-solving, and cause-and-effect sequence were easiest, and Musk taught himself how to program in three days. He sold the first software game. He created Blaster shortly after. Later, he earned his degrees in Physics and Economics, borrowed books from friends, and taught himself how to build rockets—an astonishing outlier within the *Totally^U Achiever* stage.

Even with a high academic acquisition, as much as the *Achievers* try, they cannot escape their career's purposelessness. It is not a surprise to expect individuals within the *Totally^U Achiever* stage to be happy about their lives. A *Totally^U Achiever* will immediately list their love for their job, family, and spouses. Sounds breezy to generate such a positive response! But their lives appear good. Most times, however, the opposite is true. Should we delve deeper beyond their job, family, and spouses, they would struggle to answer. Conclusion: their lives aren't *so* good after all. Hence, they feel they are within the *Totally^U Drifter* and *Totally^U Defeater* stage.

When *Achievers* appear this way, they represent the saying, "Life is just a stage." *Totally^U Achievers'* self-representations depend on how they and others in social groups see them. The superficiality of living a life within the *Totally^U Achiever* stage is through endurance. They are always in a state of either pride or shame. They worry about losing social status in others' eyes as they navigate a complex and overlapping organizational structure. *Totally^U Achievers* may have open window moments of clarity from time to time, and then there are those moments when their name is called, and they do not know how to respond.

Once *Totally^U Achievers'* aspirations and ideals are threatened and no longer congruent with their career goals and status quo, they may spend a great deal of time avoiding social disregard. A strong elicitor of shame and embarrassment. They operate from a state of mind of chance, which can quickly push them directly to the *Totally^U Drifter* stage. For *Totally^U Achievers*, survival in the real world can be their overarching motivation, and they move forward with excessive self-esteem. *Totally^U Achievers* may be caught in a bubble and do not know their reality and have little insight into how they come across to others. The outcome of a *Totally^U Achiever* stage individuals' emotion is hubristic pride, and they appear as either egotistical or arrogant.

Achievers who display these emotions sometimes live a public lie. However, it can become dangerous to live a life without discovering who you are. Ultimately, life does not differ from that of a *Totally^U Defeater*. They indulge in habits such as excessive shopping and maxed credit cards, actions intended to seduce people into believing they have a lot: the newest and the latest. *An Achiever* may also find solace in artificial stimuli, drugs, alcohol, and so on.

Each stage has positive and negative aspects; being an *Achiever* means risking blurring your personal and work identity even more than at the other stages. After meeting Troy and many other *Achievers* who have stayed within the *Totally^U Achievers* stage, every so often, I became curious. What is it about the emotional state that enables them to maintain the status quo throughout their careers? After witnessing Gerry's demise of drifting into the '*Defeated* land' from being a *Totally^U Achiever*, I stop and consider the *Totally^U Achiever's* self-conscious emotions and appraisals. Do they make their career any safer? Is any stage safe?

Yes, it's possible to make stages 'safer' with the proper guidance. And maybe "safe" may not matter as much if you look at things differently.

Chapter 8: Moment of Truth

———

Harland David Sanders is the perfect example of someone who went through all three stages—*Totally^U Drifter, Totally^U Defeater*, and *Totally^U Achiever*—multiple times over his professional life. His career shifted from Conductor to Lawyer to Insurance salesperson. Even with high-profile jobs and leaving his wife and child at his mother's residence, he constantly changed jobs to make ends meet. The cyclical demise of his career continued despite his capabilities and experience. He got to where he could not provide for his family.

It was not until Sander was sixty-three years old did, he patent his frying chicken method and launched his Kentucky Fried Chicken (KFC) brand. In no time, he expanded internationally. Sanders continuously maintained a state of mind of chance, choice, and endurance, displaying emotional agility within the varying stages. He eventually found and achieved success. Perhaps balance within the *Totally^U Achiever* stage.

"I am who I say I am." How many times have you heard this said?

It sounds assuring; however, it is not really.

You've probably stated this yourself, but if you knew why you interact the way you do and the actions of your career outcome, you would genuinely understand a significantly higher percentage of your career journey. A career is not about identity involving interpersonal, social, or public evaluation. Neither is it about your education level or accomplishments. Our current career realities make us realize that being within the *Totally^U Career Cycle* is not all-purpose and universal.

The *Totally^U Framework* represents a career phenomenon related to one's cognitive state in the person to environment fit. Making choices forces a shift from one stage level to promote behaviors that increase your emotional stability and affirm your status and roles in the organization. You are "in control" to encourage conciliation and avoidance behaviors for valued success at this basic level. To experience changes within each stage, you must form stable self-representations, direct your attention, and consciously focus on those self-representations.

The *Totally^U Achiever*, *Totally^U Drifter*, and *Totally^U Defeater* stages manifest differently in everyone. The *Totally^U Cycle* is divided into three equal offset sections. As a reminder, the *Career Cycle* is not cyclical, but that doesn't imply that it's static and that progression is linear. For example, being a *Totally^U Drifter* does not mean moving through from the *Totally^U Defender* to the *Totally^U Achiever*.

The society or circles we live within never go beyond our external. We are unprepared because our choices overwhelm our ability to manage the complex social and organizational systems we work within. Hence, we have lost our ability to filter what is important and what isn't. Instead, we let titles, a company's popularity, and other exquisite things falsely define us. Regrettably, we never see ourselves for who we are. It is a sad state to fall into this trap, yet many of us do, quitting a job before the customary three-to-six-month probationary period. What was supposed to be a dream job with the right person-environment fit becomes devastation.

Life has a strange way of catapulting us from one hundred percent to zero percent in the blink of an eye. The death of a loved one, a layoff from the dream job, a significant health issue, or a scandal can throw you off course, putting you to shame and leaving you riddled with guilt, and coupled with regrets.

Regrets throughout your career journey will emerge, and you don't have to think hard to recall a few that you experienced in the past. Regrets and doubts sit in your brain's frontal lobe, ready for recollection and to remind you to have the skill and not the will to move forward. If you do not pave the way earlier by accepting organizational mishaps, you will find yourself in the final quarter of your life without a career. The result is that you walk around drained and feel trapped at one stage, or you repetitively go through the *TotallyU Career Cycle* multiple times.

Torn apart, you can quickly move through the cycle in a spiral pattern from a *Totally^U Achiever* to a *Totally^U Defeater* or a *Totally^U Drifter* and vice versa. That is why no stage within the *Totally^U Career Cycle* is safe. By definition, the *Totally^U Career Cycle* is the natural state of your professional life represented as stages—*Totally^U Defeater, Totally^U Drifter, Totally^U Achiever.* It is assumed that emotions stemming from choice, chance and endurance have evolved through your natural career progression to facilitate survival and exponential growth.

In a structured work environment, longevity and tenure are uncertain. Therefore, we need a better understanding of ourselves to be guided through the *Totally^U Career Cycle*. The best tool available is the acquisition of self-knowledge to understand our self-conscious emotions. It is also the primary tool for making choices to evolve and exponentially grow, which is essential to promote the attainment of *Totally "U"*.

The Johari Window

O ne-way psychologists have used to explain us to ourselves and our relationship with others is through the concept of the Johari Window. The Johari Window is a fantastic model, and techniques are a window in which the 'four-pane' of our self-awareness and self-image interact. The four-panes divide our level of consciousness of our interpersonal variables that are 'open,' 'hidden, blind,' and 'unknown' at the center of the *Totally*^{U} *Career Cycle*. This accurately represents us at each stage—*Defeater, Drifter*, or *Achiever*.

This technique helps you discover your blind spots or "burners." These are how others perceive you and ultimately helps you better understand yourself. Following the premise of the Johari Window of self-awareness, presensing and co-sensing are the conversations you hold with yourself. They reflect what you learn about yourself in different areas of your life and your career. They reinforce the want to remain where you are to the unknown is a bold move.

Your burners comprise information known to others but unknown to you. Left blinded, they stay in the unconscious as it retards your growth and survival. Your 'uncomfortable truths' often cause discomfort and upset about what you tolerate in your career. Still, they instruct and righteously inform you of the bravery waiting to emerge. You either maintain or enhance your state of mind to lessen your emotional triggers and prevent the impact of workplace stressors. A career is becoming *Totally*^{U} in your professional life, possessing an authentic pride and sense of accomplishment where your confidence is accompanied by high self-worth.

With these critical questions answered, the unknowns become known, you understand what to change, and you are ready to take the next steps. You are now prepared to switch and transition to a stage that appears more balanced with your state of mind with no fuzzy lens, distortions, or shadows. This point is astoundingly unique as you purposely and deliberately dig into your personal and professional life to figure out your stage. Your insights into your hidden drivers unlock different ways of thinking, feeling, and acting as you evolve. You would have strategically eliminated what is unnecessary, and this is an indispensable requisite for your career rebirth within your stage.

You can create stability and make quantum leaps to succeed by your definition. Acquisition of self-knowledge is a primary tool for your choices.

It also becomes easier to understand how a primary emotion might promote your survival goals as you attempt to avoid the unpleasant feelings of incongruence. Once you become aware of the patterns and rhythm of your burners, you begin to ferociously ask questions, such as whether you are doing the right thing at the right time. If there is anything you deserve, it is serenity as you come closer to embodying the stage of your career—to bring a sense of calmness, free from psychological damages of colliding organizational operational strategies.

Knowing the position within the cycle that renounces your conscious emotions is an elicitation that mediates self-esteem and self-enhancement.

Chapter 9: Variants of Truth

─────

I cannot tell the number of times I have sat with clients who did not know their professional standing. Like a rudderless ship, they drift aimlessly on the ocean. Subject to the tides and winds' whims, many struggle to remain upright through no fault of their own. Their reaction is an emotional response to their unique truth.

If you have no idea who you are at the very core, an organization will lead you to depression. You feel that your personal and professional life is broken each passing day. Most aspects of your professional life comprise mutual dependencies and obligations between people and the organization. Organizations operate on what can be measured. For instance, quality, cost, and profit. While many organizations are leading workforce adoption to promote the integration of work and health, their health programs are just a "portray" of health initiatives. These are not initiatives where employees matter. Knowing who you are is pivotal in thinking, feeling, and progression through your career. Without knowing this crucial information, a part of you is missing, lonely, and alone.

Look around at your workload; your work-life balance doesn't match your performance evaluation. There is no tangible increase in your value. Organizations focus on operational value and knowledge, concentrating on metrics while not addressing your emotional state at the start of employment or throughout your tenure. Some work environments have psychometric testing administered focusing on verbal and cognitive abilities. If you are good at passing these tests, you are deemed intelligent and hired, with little attention regarding your emotional state and agility at the time of hire.

Within the *Totally^U Career Cycle*, you operate with what is open, 'hidden, blind,' and 'unknown of your unique interpersonal "burners" or interpersonal attributes. This means that for each burner, the angle of reflection is a percentage of reality bouncing off at the same angle of our individual truth. How you understand and respond when the burners are triggered determines how quickly you transition from the less desired stage to the more desired.

The overwhelming majority of us learn, live, and love within all our burners at the center of the *Totally^U Framework*. Your burners conflict with each other as the angle of reflection bounces off in the same direction. Your self-identity reflects your social identities, your career, and your vocation.

Ego and self-esteem lie in another plane, equally your passion and your purpose. This represents a percentage of your reality and varnished truth. These interpersonal attributes are the determining factors on how quickly the transition is made from the less desired stage to the more desired stage. These burners are the primary cause of the psychological challenges that affect your encounters as a *Defeater, Drifter,* or an *Achiever*. They are the root of what leads to the creation of confusion, alongside insatiability, clearness, self-assurance, and gratification. In a nutshell, the variants of your personal truth create a balance and trade-off of your burners at each stage of the cycle.

The Right Flow

———

M oving from stage to stage is more or less an emotional state. A stage change can leave you feeling frustrated and excited all at the same time, as a shift from one stage to another does not guarantee arrival at your desired stop. We often see qualified people fired, not for knowledge and skill, but an attitude that develops from the recurring patterns that become habits formed by their state of mind. Maybe you need to turn off the sound and take time to listen to your self-aggrandizing remarks and believe your pseudo-self-depreciating remarks are not true. Something will die with each rebirth, and something new is reborn in each stage.

All stages are valid as you self-actualize and better understand your experiences along the *Totally^U Career Cycle*. Hence, the more reason to become self-conscious and aware of your burners. And as you do so, the process and a healthy state of mind will manifest into your personal life and professional career. Integrating your self-identity, ego, passion, and purpose reveals some of the deepest patterns running through the relationships between each attribute and each stage, especially as we live in an unpredictable, fast-paced world and within colliding organizational systems.

Just as your present values and beliefs may not be different to when you first entered the *Totally^U Career Cycle*, so is your emotional state. Therefore, to reduce the friction of executing in your professional life, your best option is emotional management as a coping strategy for your state of mind. Hence, I cannot stress enough that first, you need to be honest with yourself and find your truth as a *Totally^U Drifter*,

Totally^U Defeater, or a *Totally^U Achiever*. Then gauge your responsive progression as all attributes rest with applauding honesty with yourself.

The *Totally^U Framework* allows you to align and clarify what is possible for your full professional intent and potential. This means stretching beyond what feels natural and creating mental imagery of your future state. Not only will you gain absolute clarity, but you will also become fully mobilized to achieve something truly excellent. When you are competently conscious at the correct gauge, you become more adaptable to effectuate change. Only you can determine the direction for your person-to-environment maintenance behavior.

A chance to find your stage within the *Totally^U Career Cycle* is not a fathomable mystery. Frankly, most individuals do not gain the initiative to change their stage because of mental burnout. Therefore, they become comfortable with the uncomfortable and dislike change. Yet, it is worth the effort. A failure to confront leads to frustration and results in a continual shift, an imbalance, and you remain stagnant within the *Career Cycle*.

Once you understand the issues of your burners at hand, the result is a solution rather than withdrawal from the trigger emotions of the work environment. You meet it head-on and avoid repeating the unwanted reaction, which could further reveal each stage's inadequacies. This is superb in a good way. It is difficult as you experience emotional discomfort at work. It takes daily prayer to stay in a job that will not lead you into depression.

It takes courage, insight, and foresight to see which activities and efforts will add to your single highest point of the contribution that influences your professional life. It takes asking yourself tough questions and making real trade-offs. Exercising severe discipline cuts out the competing priorities that distract your true career intentions.

Engaging in genuine sustained connection and generative dialogue with yourself also takes practice to find emotional balance in a *Totally U* Career. Do not worry about making the wrong choice. As you go through the *Totally^U Career Cycle*, each stage will look different; sometimes balanced, another time imbalanced. This state of flux will drive you away or towards your future emotional state. Your future self and career come into play to guide your internal drive to revolve or evolve within the *Totally^U Career Cycle*. Those who choose to embrace the discomfort of connecting with the self, and reflect on the process, find themselves in an expansive state. Whether you call it enlightenment or a metamorphosis, it is an awakening of the psychological response to adapt to your work environment that alters your state of mind and changes your stage.

The urgency of going through the *Totally^U Career Cycle* depends on your current work situation. It depends on your wants and how quickly you want to move to your future state—as the unseen is now seen and the unknown becomes known. The decision you make is up to you. The process from your more profound understanding of the elements of your consciousness of your burners all shapes how you show up. It shines a light on your evolutionary development and states of consciousness. These crucial elements are required to learn to trust your intuition and prepare to discover and process your emotions.

Maybe what I am sharing about the variants of your truth is not for you. The decision you make to become accountable to yourself is the first step if you want to reveal the side of your unknown or unseen. You are about to touch, taste, and smell your way to a career that is balanced and figured out. By processing your emotions for passion and purpose alongside your ego, self-identity, and other non-personal attributes, you can determine your person-to-environment and maintenance behavior within the *Totally^U Career Cycle*.

Chapter 10: The Burden Bearer

———

Meet Alex, my former manager. He is the typical reflection of ego and self-esteem burner.

To drive a sense of "self," he was the first item on the agenda in every meeting. He needed to take center stage. His opening remarks became a nursery rhyme to how he started the company. If someone arrived late, the meeting would start over. Once we moved past an exhausting sixty minutes, he became the language construct police, always having to be correct. The type of person who disregarded the opinions and input of others, he was always one to make statements and decisions based solely on what he wanted. If a team member said the sky is blue today, he'd respond, *"technically, the sky is blue but a light shade of blue. That does not make it the mother of the blue family."* He was not consciously aware of how he came across to the team. It was no surprise that we were happy when our meeting ended, and a tremendous sense of relief descended. We had survived his ego—his prominent "I" and "me" figure and a meeting he thought effective.

E-G-O is a small three-letter word capable of destroying your professional life as it manifests itself in false pride. The ego has a significant construct. It is both the conscious and the deep subconscious level of your mind with the whole construct similar to a gigantic iceberg. Most of the depth of the iceberg is submerged in the ocean. Similarly, the ego lies in the depth of your subconscious and becomes something unseen. Those we encounter only see the tip of it. This small percent at the conscious level is how we manifest ourselves.

The ego is significant because, as career professionals, survivability and identity in the workplace depend on achieving your goals and on how you master the task to accomplish those goals.

As your professional identity forms from achieving organizational goals, internal evaluation activates, and your emotional association is beyond reproach and infallibility in goal attainment. However, this self-appraisal for goal attainment comes with shame, pride, or guilt—leaving one small, inferior, helpless, and exposed. So, when feelings of tension, regret, or remorse kick in, questions will emerge.

Am I flawed?

Was the failed organizational outcome my fault?

Was it my intellectual level or competence?

Your hubristic or authentic pride will determine how you process these emotions. People with big egos exalt themselves, while bruised or inferior egos may suffer shame and insecurity. These are implicit and explicit emotional responses related to beliefs about your competence and motivation to achieve your goals. For example, if you are a positive person and goals are not fulfilled, your self-worth remains intact after an emotional evaluation with positive belief. These beliefs genuinely build your self-confidence and develop your skills to promote achievement.

In contrast, a negative belief may impair you if you strive for high standards, and the motivation for a self-enhancing quest for status and dominance drives you. You may see yourself as a failure when you do not achieve goals. After all, motivation for this self-enhancing quest for status and dominance is strong. For individuals with an unhealthy ego, within the $Totally^U$ Achiever stage, the organization's survival and performance can become overarching. Their thoughts and emotions can become excessive, and they are unaware of how they come across to others.

We may catch *Totally*^{U} *Drifters* and *Totally*^{U} *Achievers* in a bubble displaying a bigger-than-the-earth attitude and not knowing their reality. Therefore, ego and self-esteem become relevant for goal performance and is congruent with professional representation. Hence, the ego is part of the personality that mediates the demands of reality.

Your ego influences your thoughts, motives, emotions, behavior, and, ultimately, your personality. Your personality is not who you are. However, the word personality is susceptible to misrepresentation, speaking of habits adopted that have become a behavior. Neither are you an introvert, ambivert, or extrovert. Personality develops from previous trauma in many ways, and when suppressed trauma heals, personality can change. Your personality shows up in certain situations and relationships when the moralistic part of the personality formed in childhood conflicts with current social influences.

Every so often, a career professional can enter a work environment that they felt was their dream job and the right fit. After a few months, that dream job becomes a place to hide your soul to limit the psychological impact. This creates an imbalanced ego. Pride allows the ego to take center stage, and self-evaluation is favorable, making thoughts, motives, emotions, and behaviors infused with "me" and "I."

When this accumulates over time, it is channeled in a way that identifies with who you are, how you live, and where you work. This is consistent with the compromise models of career choice, where integrated career interactions develop into self and ego identity. Likewise, you change at each stage of the *Totally*^{U} *Career Cycle* to adapt to your career over time.

The Need for Perfection

C areer professionals feel pride when attention is on them, and these feelings are attached to their specific behavior for mastery of goals for personal and organizational outcomes. The need for this mastery of goals triggers a strive for perfectionism and self-esteem and ensuing issues. Stemming from the constant emotional anguish of shame and guilt in both private and public self-representation and where public transgression leads to self-conscious emotions of shame. In contrast, a private transgression leads to guilt. Failure to achieve one's workplace goals endangers a set of unrealistic social, personal, and familial standards and expectations and drives unattainable ideal self-identity.

The need for perfectionism increases self-esteem by enhancing "self-competence" and "self-acceptance." Perfectionism becomes about providing for the self and, therefore, serves the ego. Hence, perfectionists career professionals are often insecure and anxious about falling short of their standards. They are very self-critical and unhappy and often suffer from low self-esteem. As a result, they constantly live in fear of private shame, and public humiliation as their desire to outperform their peers motivates them to exceed performance standards. They also try to avoid "looking dumb." Such adaptive perfectionism is associated with conscientiousness and task-specific self-confidence towards personal and professional goal achievement.

A character trait that is distinguishable across the *Totally^U Career Cycle* stages is the career professional with high self-esteem that strives for high standards to improve their competence when they do not achieve goals. Contrary to a deficient achievement goal, an abundant self-representation maximizes pride by continually inflating positive representation of performance outcomes. This is a frequent validation for suppressing shame and what we call false pride.

When correlated with a shameful reaction, this biased self-assessment and low self-esteem results in negative emotions. Emotions lead to depression, stress, suicidal ideation, hopelessness, and other dysfunctional coping mechanisms such as withdrawal and disengagement and transcend professional life into personal life.

The Awakened Ego

E veryone has their own set of preferences for interacting with the world around them. So, close relationships are pivotal in the development of self-esteem. Your ego's degree will differ. The habits formed are the ones to be mindful of the excessive egocentric viewpoint encapsulated in "me" and "I"—frames of reference for feeding the ego. Since the ego is based on self-representation, it can easily be distorted as it merges with your self-identity. For instance, you may perceive yourself as invaluable while not defining yourself as valuable, creating two different constructs. Therefore, it is essential to focus on having a balanced ego when creating your self-identity.

The first step to balance your ego is identifying when it is not serving your career. As when the ego is controlled, your professional life awakens. Solidifying this argument is learning to live in this world with deep core values and learning not to see reality from your illusion. As you understand how the ego works in your work environment, you can use it healthily without becoming egotistical, selfish, or insecure. Many empathic and servant leaders show this.

When the product development team needed to present the company's product offering, my former manager, Alex, resorted to defending his self-identity. His hubristic ego became the focus of the occasion. Instead of the company's boardroom, Alex resorted to a suite with spectacular ocean views and a balcony that extended the length of the suite at a five-star hotel. He informed the Hotel Manager to stage the suite for a boardroom where floor-to-ceiling glass doors provided refreshing scenery to watch the yachts cruise past on the Intracoastal Waterway. The atmosphere was everything until Alex's ego showed up and conformed to the demands of his current reality—his, me, myself, and I.

He exaggerated his significance and importance in the company, acting as though there was a threat and a dire need to fight for retreat. He considered himself separate and different from his team at that moment. This move prevented him from placing ink on the paper, and he lost a lucrative business contract. This contract would have given his company a powerful vantage point in the technology industry.

Ego problem is attributed to low self-esteem—not having pride in yourself. When career professionals have no clarity, they develop low self-esteem and do not have confidence-resulting in a big ego to imitate poise. The longer you leave it, the more it manifests itself into an imbalance of making every day solely on subjective internal motivation. When dealing with your ego, it is great to find a sense of balance instead of trying to suppress it or destroy it. Understanding ego means there will be a need to change how you act. It starts with co-sensing. Presencing allows you to take a step outside your perspective. It helps you see things from other viewpoints, some that do not always support your own reality.

High self-esteem acknowledges individual limitations. A healthy ego is not afraid to show vulnerability and does not need constant validation while maintaining a firm sense of self-worth and competence. In turn, a healthy ego connects to a healthy self-identity.

Chapter 11: The Twins

———

The meaning of one's career reminds me of an anecdote I once heard. Three people worked to break up rocks. When asked about the purpose behind their actions, the first replied, "Making a living." The second responded, "Making little ones out of big ones," and the third said, "Building a cathedral." These framed responses reflect the individual subjectivity of work and how it contributes to your physical, cognitive, and emotional presence in a fully functioning performance role. There is more to life than just having a job.

You formed most of your career aspirations in your early life. Take the time to think back and reflect. From as early as five years old, others frequently may have asked, "What do you want to be when you grow up?" And more often than not, you replied with a knowingness that belied your years. However, throughout the years, your interests changed, and schools kept you busy with academic subjects considered "important."

As you begin your working years, you approach the *Totally^U Career Cycle*, with an expectation of having a career "flow." One that sits somewhere between your early childhood aspirations and areas of study. Yet, a construct overlap may occur when comparing a career with a vocation and work-related norms. A set of social expectations regulate your social interaction and influence the meaning work has for you. As a result, a tide of emotional waves emerges between practicality and romanticism as you approach work.

As the *Career Cycle* turns, there are a set of problematic twin burners in your professional life. A construct overlap occurs between having a career and a vocation, and this is where people get confused the most within the three stages of the *Totally^U Career Cycle*. For example, you can identify with the drifter stage, as you are unsure when you are in the right career. You might lack purpose within the *Defeater* stage, and getting to an *Achiever* stage, only to realize you were leaning along the wrong wall throughout all of your careers. Exploring and discovering which job you will do is perhaps one of the most critical ethical decisions you can make.

Vocation and career are powerful paradigms—the ideal versus reality. Troy, the Firefighter who has the career which he discerned from an early age, his ideal is his reality. A career is an implicit and explicit selection you made when you started working to promote your professional identity development, interpersonal development, and personal meaning for financial compensation.

Careers' visible representations of work effectiveness follows a series of choices, sets of preferences, goal attainments, and an increasing level of responsibility or learning with each successive job position. Depending on the stage you find yourself within the *Totally^U Career Cycle*, your career focuses primarily on the foreseen value in the marketplace. The secondary is the series of educational activities of having professional skills. Supporting the premise of the *Totally^U Framework,* careers develop, change, and accumulate over time for exponential professional growth or decay.

Unlike a career where it would be easy for you to quit, a vocation does not feel like a choice and is less central to your self-identity. It is more reliant on where you find meaningfulness and experience social contribution. Vocations manifest in personal actions rather than external rewards. They are a work role where you put in more than what you get out. Vocation is what Carl Jung, Psychoanalyst, describes as the "voice of the inner man."

A vocation is something that nourishes your entire life and characterizes how you operate in your non-work life. Career professionals who have discovered their vocation are committed to or even become obsessed with their careers. Austin Russell, Luminar Founder and CEO, the youngest self-made billionaire, displays an unrelenting obsession for his vocation. He dropped out of Stanford University to focus on LIDAR technology for enabling autonomous cars–this transpired as an emotional experience he found incredible and surreal.

Understanding the *Totally*^{U} *Career Cycle* and your morals embedded into every high-priority decision you make creates a heightened awareness, and a motivation to be intentional and find your vocation instead of a career.

The Carryover Effect

———

We tend to think everything is straightforward with our career until our professional life takes on a whole different meaning. It is the usual pattern to begin on an occupational path that you believe is suitable, but you become disconnected or disengaged from it somewhere along the journey. There are cues when you examine your career aspirations and preferences, core values and the constraining forces imposed by the social environment you work in. Your career choice becomes a complex process because you face an effort to clarify and implement a series of work-related decisions over time. So, you pursue a career that is not a sum of your decisions. Over time, that can be favorable, or the job you choose may not be a good place for your existence. This is where your twin—vocation and career plays more of a role in career choice.

The realization that you have begun something that you are not suited for drives you to seek ways to find an alternative direction to commit to instead. As you pursue meaning in your professional life, regret or remorse problems show as the feeling of tension builds conflict in your minds. Here, you find yourself at a place where you suffer from neurosis and repeated instances of striking out on your dream and riding out working for a paycheck. It becomes easy to see a clear distinction between the two constructs of a vocation and career.

Working a career without having a vocation produces a *Carryover Effect* that negatively impacts other parts of your life. Sometimes, it is no fault of your own, especially in the labor market, where constraints and opportunities provided by your demographic location modify your early career hopes and dreams.

As a professional, you may approach your work in a way that resembles a vocation, making career orientations into an over-represented work role. For example, information from the LinkedIn survey showed a breach of the implied contract with an employer over guaranteed psychological safe employment in assumed roles. Therefore, we see individuals within the *Totally^U Drifter* and *Totally^U Defeater* stage reporting lower job satisfaction, lower job performance, more job stress, and shorter tenure. Conversely, career professionals who approach work as a vocation, such as Troy, the firefighter, have more clarity, greater self-identity, less stress, depression, and more extraordinary professional life satisfaction.

The career professional within the *Totally^U Achiever* stage who chooses a service-oriented career and has a genuine vocation will see difficulties as challenges. And they grow professionally to learn from and develop continually from such experiences. *Totally^U Drifter Stage* professionals who select a career as a vocation because it is a relatively secure profession will lack commitment. They find a vocation to fill a void that often transforms them into drained, stressed, and exhausted individuals.

If the behavior or environment does not change, those within the *Totally^U Drifter* stage find themselves within the *Totally^U Defeater* stage. Likewise, *Totally^U Achiever* career professionals drift or down rightly get defeated. As painful as the experience can sometimes be, it represents a significant opportunity to change.

Despite what you have achieved in your career or vocation, you may still go through the motion of being unfulfilled. For instance, you may fail at a project to make a difference in your community or environmental interest and become hard on yourself. Career experiences can be quite distinct from and unrelated to each other, but they still link up. There are thoughts, feelings, desires, goals, hopes, and motivation that produces a *Carryover Effect*. There is no on-off switch of one experience into the next, and the very recent past can bleed into the occurring present and become problematic to move forward.

A residue in your personal life affects your subsequent experience in subtle yet powerful ways. It is an inherent part of your career that cannot be ignored. Instead, they must be embraced deliberately, strategically, and thoughtfully. When a career choice is in sync with a vocation, it increases your chances of experiencing the highest growth within the *Totally^{U} Career Cycle*. This feels like a more natural progression between your current stage to the desired outcome at any stage.

Chapter 12: Know Thyself

———

Standing on my little stool behind the counter, I watched keenly as my Aunt Ty placed her customer's order. My aunt told me to pack the grocery shopping bag with the unique sign language we had developed between us. On days when I was bullied with the "dummy" label placed firmly upon me, my aunt's small grocery was my school. This was the perfect place and a better place to avoid the demoralization of my label. Too many passionately believed the unfounded assumption that I was a "dummy" compared to others. But in my aunt's shop, my world was different. I was receiving real-life teaching with my mother's sister. This was a blessing for my mother, who had eight other children to care for and a class of twenty-six students to teach.

As a child, the only self-identity I had was programmed by the label placed on me within the school environment. I was a girl. I was born in Jamaica. I was a dummy. But I became fixated on the beautiful job I was doing as Aunty Ty's assistant. With each customer's grocery bag I packed, this label became less important in my new learning environment. She confirmed my worth with her warm smile and the dialogue that was special between us. I was understood and appreciated in a role in my environment that mattered.

I felt my job was significant, and I was important.

For most people, there is nothing more important to your sense of identity than your career. After all, your work is where you spend most of your twenty-four, waking-hours each day. As adults, when you meet people for the first time, the question that follows your name most often is, "What do you do?" Here, your new acquaintance is assessing and making assumptions about your profession and achievements.

You are not a detached observer from your answer. Your answer is one that is tied up in the significance of your job. How it projects with your feelings of importance is tied to one's identity. Your identity is not limited by your thoughts, feelings, or dreams. Your identity extends well beyond the confines of identifiers, personality traits, abilities, physical attributes, aspirations, and others that make you who you are.

Here, reference is made to your deep core beliefs of your self-identity, related to your social environment, and how you function within that context. One that gives your identity dynamics its importance in defining who you are—the financial status, social status, or perhaps health status. Within the *Totally^U Cycle*, self-identity is who you see or define yourself to be, and this collective representation is based on self-attachment and congruent environmental fit. Without knowing your self-identity, you are subject to the whims of the tides and winds of a rudderless ship drifting on the ocean.

Attachment to Labels

L ike a sponge, you have soaked up years of your identity based on cultural reality and the social labels that society places on you. When taken together, there are different identity construct possibilities, which may differ over time: job seeker, employee, father, mother, coach, leader. One of the most common injustices you can do to yourself is to tie your self-identity firmly to your job title.

You are not your job.

Your job title is nothing more than a symbolic encounter with an organization. It is a concept that is developed based on common assumptions and serves only as a representation of the role and not you. An attached label to your job can become a sense of attachment security for inner gratification. This awareness develops the minute you enter the *Totally^U Cycle*.

Social identity is always in force and attached to a company and its subcultures. It serves for adaptive and status cohesion with the organization and your coworkers. If you are within the Totally^U Drifter stage, you will have changed jobs a few times throughout your career. And so powerful is a title, that after a time, people become somewhat unwilling to accept job positions that contradict their social identity.

A job title can disappear for many reasons throughout your career years. Without separating labels from your true identity, you risk experiencing negative emotions regardless of the stage you find yourself in. Take Tessa as an example. She was within the *Totally^U Achiever* stage and the epitome of success, and her self-identity was tied up so close to the role she performed. So, when made redundant, she lost her sense of pride and felt embarrassed. She was lost as she could no longer attach to the social status identified with the company, she had worked with for over thirty-five years. She struggled to find her self-identity.

Once you are grouped within a particular social hierarchy, you embody the physical representation, language, and communication grounded in job titles. Career professionals approach their jobs to the relative value or the social standing of their role within their work environment and with their coworkers. For instance, the Office Assistant may be seen as having a higher social class than a Janitorial Aide, but compared with the District Manager, an Office Manager will have a lower social standing.

Instead, you have a keen sense of social hierarchy and the social status you want to be associated with, irrespective of where you work. This can be seen as an individual strategy to overcome the transition to a *Totally^U Defeater*. As a *Totally^U Drifter*, you strive for improvement as you seek the ultimate social standing of the *Totally^U Achiever*. Similarly, if you are a *Totally^U Achiever*, you will protect and maintain your "privileged" position through competition and creativity.

Identity is as personal as it is social. Social and cultural autobiographical memories and narratives are also highly relational to how your symbolic representations are derived—both in content and form. For example, prominent successful figures, whose identity, and story narratives are crafted and portrayed in enhanced imagery of success. As career professionals, some of us seek to be the Elon Musk or Jeff Bezos.

As professionals within the *Totally^U Defeater*, *Totally^U Drifter*, and *Totally^U Achiever*, you can spend your energy hiding your vulnerabilities to become a person who doesn't even matter. It is essential that you do not camouflage yourself to fit with the cultural and organizational milieu. These successes are not blueprints. They leave clues. They are far-reaching, subtle self-fulfilling prophecy effects as you tell your career story to others or ask their opinions about possible future identities. It is a ramification that affects everything else and consequently intertwines with your lives, relationships, marriages, and families.

Attachment to Place

The subtleties of language are not reflected by the impact they may have. I do not mean to turn detective, but have you ever noticed what happens when opening a conversation about a job? The job title precedes the organization. For example, when you ask, "What is your occupation?" I am a Product Manager at Amazon emphasizes the organization. The respondent does not see themselves as just a "Product Manager," they positively distinguish their employer from other "relevant companies." These are based on perceived value, and this is the individual's presumed dimensions and the worth of their comparison.

The same is true for individuals who share the same nationality. There is a vast difference between looking good and creating a body cult compared to creating a shallow soul and identifying with people who belong in a place. I frequently come across my countryman and enquire where on the island they grew up. Of course, they associate themselves with an urban city rather than a rural town. Obsession with social identity is one conflict that can cost us our values. This is especially in a society where social comparison, and particularly in response to social media standards of achievement, is so prominent. The result is a significant crisis that provokes and threatens our self-identity.

Just as people defend their characters against threats to personal self-esteem or self-integrity, career professionals similarly engage in a wide range of social identity maintenance strategies. It is these strategies that may help restore positive organization distinctiveness when one is threatened or undermined. The reptile brain takes charge, eliciting behavior such as stereotyping and social status or influence.

Such self-concept can affect how you negotiate, and especially how you negotiate information about yourself.

Gerry, the C-Suite Executive, is a good example. His self-understanding was pronounced in the strengths of the adjectives he used to judge why he was within the $Totally^U$ *Defeater* stage. His judgement showed high levels of anxiety and nonconstructive behaviors. These behaviors impact individuals within the $Totally^U$ *Drifter* and the $Totally^U$ *Defeater* stage ability to recover and revise his or her self-image in the face of severe work environment constraints.

Totally^U Crossover

The self-identity quadrant is unique in that your self-identity gives a sense of "wholeness"—Totally "U". When expanded or contracted over time, your energy and consciousness create a behavior pattern that determines your current state within the cycle. Your experiences throughout the cycle are both expected and unanticipated. As you do not choose the groups or organizations you work in, it is not also limited to your present. Most of us change and develop throughout our lifetimes, and just as our values and beliefs at present may not be what they were in the past, your self-identity can also include your future self. This is an explicit prospection of whom you want to become.

Mastering and understanding this burner is both interesting and critical because if you don't know your true identity, you seek validation from systems and people who place little value or importance of you as an individual. Then there is no way you can be your authentic self. However, a heightened awareness enables you to control your unlimited potential for finding purpose, satisfaction, and balance in any given *Totally^U* stage. And this remains consistent beyond personality assessment and organizational metrics.

Self-identity and social identity are at every stage of the *Totally^U Cycle*. As your career matures, your deep core values are needed to provide a stable foundation in your professional life and shape your views. Therefore, the role you play is crucial to how you think, how you feel, and go about your day-to-day life at work. It is not the label your family tells you are—nor your job title from your place of work. Self-understanding is needed for a transformational experience to become Totally U, and therefore, you must be intentional and disregard information perpetuated by ignorance

Chapter 13 Purposefully Passionate

———

As we clarify and implement a series of career decisions, the process becomes complex. We question the paradigms of our passion and purpose burner. The meaning you give to work is formed by the decisions taken to balance personal characteristics with societal constraints. It is a continuous process that evolves within the *Totally^U Career Cycle* as you evaluate the meaningfulness of your contribution to the organization's job function. It is an intrinsic desire extending beyond career choice and an organizational wall. The grades, diplomas, and or references alone do not lead to the fulfillment of meaningfulness through your career.

Instead, we choose jobs that accumulate over our careers, becoming masters of many trades. We commonly hear the phrase "Jack of all trades." It is hardly aspirational when we become "masters of none" of our gained trades. However, it should never be entertained that doing everything is a limitation. It was considered well-versed to understand multiple different disciplines in the renaissance period. It does not differ from the many people within the *Totally^U Career Cycle*, who is a success by society's definition and see work for only a paycheck. Yet, they search for and do not currently have a sense of purpose in the work they do.

I, too, was out and floating within the *Totally^U Drifter* stage for an exceptionally long time, trying to find my purpose. I searched within myself, trying to understand the fragments of a mismatch between my varying roles within my work environment and life purpose. Each time I came up empty.

Later on in life, it all made sense. Not being able to speak early and able to pursue many creative interests became my super bloc. My career came together with every lesson learned complemented by the other to find my purpose. Finally, I realized that life's pursuit is to come to purpose. The waste of life is to miss that purpose.

Throughout a career journey, when trying to connect work with an overall sense of purpose in the world is where you may get confused and lost. Unfortunately, this is also where you strike out on your career dream. As such, you may find yourself always either in the "presence of" or "in the search for" meaning. The real challenge for purpose and passion is between work-related values and their influence on your moral compass developed throughout your life—the ones from your social conditioning and a conviction of your gathered beliefs. The variations of your truth affirm your current reason for your reality. For example, having a job to pay the bills is not the *purpose* but a reason for which you work.

Purpose plays more of a significant role in your career identity than the mere stable transactional relationship from employment. The choices from an individual and organizational perspective of a wrong person-environment relationship leads to a lack of meaningfulness. Work should facilitate purpose, meaning, and self-actualization. Especially when you spend most of your wake hours at work. This is a unique motivation that should persuade you to enhance your abilities towards your purpose. If not, mindfulness of a wrong person-environment relationship leads to repeated occurrences of self-defeating behaviors.

Purposeful living is expressed as a generative stage of life and a desirable end-state for emotional safety and a contribution to others' well-being.

"Making your mark" is to make an impact other than to sustain your basic need for food, water, and shelter for your existence on earth. This appears commonsense and manifests itself in Colossians 3:23-24 (KJV), where the Apostle Paul tells us, "Whatever you do, work at it with all your heart, as working for the Lord, not for human masters, since you know you will receive an inheritance from the Lord as a reward." While it may be extremely difficult, or perhaps impossible, as we try to derive any sense of purpose from a job, the activities from work are among several factors which contribute to intolerance of our state of mind in the pursuit of meaning.

Experiencing meaningfulness and purpose in a work role is not just for the privileged. Some aspects of work may exist alongside negative and positive outcomes as individuals complete their work.

For example, you may try to account for your career trajectory and discover your life has a purpose. However, those who continually experience career-related negative influences of unpleasant physical and mental actions, such as ongoing workplace discrimination, barriers to pay benefits and prestige, sexism, racism, and economic necessity, are less likely to find purpose in their work.

After migrating from Jamaica to the United States of America, I had an interesting share of this reality. Racism was new to me. We were taught that our country's motto—Out of many one people—was a significant tribute to the unity of the different cultural minorities inhabiting our country from childhood. Classism was more prevalent, equating the poor, or the less educated citizens with disadvantages. After incidences of racism, my conclusion is that classism is generational, but classism could get better with time, support, and academic sacrifice. My skin color that led to racial remarks was natural and traced back to our DNA. I cannot change the color of my skin. However, I can fix classism. So, I go to school, follow the rules, study, get a well-paying job and work hard to climb the corporate ladder. As I approached the *Career Cycle*, the rules changed. I didn't change them. So did my state of mind.

Working in a corporate environment, I realized economic gains and a rise in social mobility is embedded in some organizational structures. They are subtle and rarely discussed. It is *the white elephant in the room*. Oppression starts and appears when in the areas of recruitment and promotion. As career professionals of color, we are less likely to grow in our professional life. It could be my choice to change the stage. Otherwise, I endure the inequality of racism or hope that the organization adopts a culture of egalitarianism by chance. We need psychological and physiological mastery of our resilience, commitment, and persistence to significantly influence ourselves to move past this demoralizing experience.

Many career professionals also face extreme and forced conditions at work that are antithetical to experiencing meaningful work. For instance, individuals with jobs low on the prestige hierarchy positions may have entered the workplace from economic necessity rather than as the result of an unconstrained career decision-making process.

Fresh out of college, Joan accepted an administrative position at a Tobacco Manufacturing Company. Because of the job market, she experienced an inter-role conflict of spirituality, family, and work—elements that provided a cornerstone of her wellbeing of being *Totally U*. Demographic and economic barriers prevented her from seeking other organizations as a preferred career choice. These choices remained beyond her control. She unhappily endured her work environment. In Joan's circumstance, a lack of resources was a barrier to discovering a purpose, a source of motivation to self-explore and try out different kinds of work. That is why some individuals in other countries of the world never find meaningfulness in their work. They instead reframe their existing work responsibilities in a way that transforms their work into purpose.

Sandy, a migrant worker, made a 360-degree career transition from a server at a five-star restaurant to a janitorial aide. She crafted her career story of what she considered her otherwise undesirable job in a way that encouraged her to contribute to her coworker's hygiene and a broader purpose that enhanced public health safety. Rather than the actual nature of the job choice and an extrinsic motivation towards a high salary and benefits, the hardship faced as an immigrant facilitated the pursuit of her purpose. For her, this was the promotion of public health measures. Career professionals within the *Totally^U Career Cycle* who endorse power, prestige, and wealth accumulations are less likely to find their work purposeful. There is no substitute for discovering what you like doing and living out your purpose.

Passionate on Purpose

There is a big difference between being a workaholic and fulfilling organizational commitment; in the same way, there is a difference between obsession for work and working harmoniously. These are two diverse thoughts. The two passion constructs of working obsessively and harmoniously share similarities with work engagement. Among them are work-related symptoms of burnout, turnover intentions, quality of interpersonal relationships, meaningfulness, and belongingness at work. Fulfilling work activities emerge from a controlled internalization of organizational or personal pressure to achieve goals. This helps explain why some individuals with a strong inclination towards goal attainment are more satisfied with an appraisal of their job or work experiences. This need leads to committing to harmonious work for a purpose-filled career.

However, an obsession with mastering work activities takes on an overbearing place in one's self-identity. Career professionals within the *Totally^U Drifter* stage who are harmoniously passionate about work can choose to engage freely and disengage from work because of belongingness and other social inclinations. In contrast, individuals within the *Totally^U Achiever* stage who are obsessively passionate about work may feel compelled to engage in work activities, causing them to ruminate about work when not on the work clock.

A *Totally^U Defeater* may lack passion about the work they undertake. Being harmoniously passionate positively affects job satisfaction, providing good mental and physical health and high self-esteem. These positive emotions promote a broadening of self-awareness, and there is more employee engagement to foster stronger social bonds and togetherness. This is an essential context for both the individual and the organization. Increased knowledge about the factors through which passion increases or restricts satisfaction with work can aid employers in their efforts to improve employees' job motivation and performance.

Everyone has a central life purpose of being fulfilled through one's work. Some people spend a year, while some spend twenty years exploring their purpose, while others can easily live and articulate their purpose. For example, Elon Musk lived and breathed his vision and was relentless in his quest to drive his business ventures forward. Fellow employees recall how he'd choose to sleep on the floor under his desk, with no pillow at the sound of banging metal in his Tesla manufacturing plant. Sleep was necessary to achieve his purpose and was not a reward for him. He is a case in point of a career professional passionate about purpose.

Hoping to find equilibrium, most career professionals I engage with approach their professional life between career and vocation and purpose and passion. This is where peace of mind resides, as clarity of these two explicit mirror image interpersonal attributes places you in the best position to be *Totally U*. At the end of your career journey or retirement, the impact and how you harmonized your space of work and whether you continued chasing the path led you to a dead end.

Chapter 14: Monsters in the Closet

━━━

So, you've taken the big decision to change things in your professional life many times, and in your mind, you have a coherent plan of action. In theory, your professional life will improve. Yet, other factors are outside of your control, and these trigger your emotions. As humans, we are terrible at figuring out emotions. We become a walking bundle of miscalculations, contradictions, and irrationalities.

Just like a movie with multiple acts, you will act in various roles at each stage of the *Totally^U Career Cycle* you find yourself in. There are shadowing effects that come to the fore that cannot be ignored. Specifically fear, the thoughts of actions yet to emerge. Fear's reality shapes how we think consciously and subconsciously about our career path and threatens our peace of mind.

Foe of Fear

With FEAR, the conceptual relationship we build up in our heads will exploit and control us. FEAR is the preconceived shaping of what we think, what we say, and what we do. Sometimes for the better, most other times for the worse. Think about your own career journey. At each stage of the cycle, fear creeps up, making it impossible to imitate or apply everything you experience at any one stage of the $Totally^U$ *Career Cycle* with another.

For example, the fear experienced within the $Totally^U$ *Achiever* stage is not the same fear expressed in $Totally^U$ *Drifter* or the $Totally^U$ *Defeater* stage. For instance, career professionals within the $Totally^U$ *Achievers* stage fear losing their social status, whereas *Drifter* stage individuals may fear not finding their passion and life purpose. Meanwhile, the *Defeater* stage career professionals may see fear sinking an individual deeper into their career demise.

Fear can dominate. The vast number of different things career professionals are afraid of within the workplace is implausible. Every day, there is the fear of failure, disappointment, embarrassment, loss of truth, having a voice, loneliness, acceptance, imperfections, leaving a job to pursue a passion, and the fear of not having a purpose in a chosen field of study. This never-ending list creates real obstacles and keeps individuals within the $Totally^U$ *Drifter*, $Totally^U$ *Defeater*, or $Totally^U$ *Achiever* stage.

The consequence reaches a point where confidence is eroded, and there is no certainty of the direction along the $Totally^U$ *Career Cycle*. Then, commitment challenges enter the fear dilemma. For instance, being within the *Totally^U Drifter* stage, the fear of embarrassment transpires as individuals play it safe by going with the flow. This motivates them to compromise what they think is necessary to be accepted by others. Within the *Totally^U Achiever* stage, individuals may be overwhelmed by increased responsibilities but remain caught up in the fear of losing their social status.

The similarities on each stage for individuals that experience fear within the *Totally^U Career Cycle* include quitting jobs or remaining paralyzed by safety in the known, or rather than exploring the unknown and continuing to fight for survival.

We form predispositions and assumptions about our career experiences that do not reflect our reality as we are tested. Instead, we constantly filter information, shaping our perceived experience. This means that the residue of the recent past can influence how we interpret a new situation, behave in it, the choices we make, and our emotions. We take our current work situation's context and background information and form a new present reality in our daily work roles. Our mind lingers in fear of the recent past before it gradually moves into the new situation or desired stage of a *Totally^U Drifter*, *Totally^U Defeater*, or *Totally^U Achiever*. Consequently, these fears eventually alter and become a part of our identity.

In instances, *Totally^U Achievers* can still face the fear of keeping self-identity in alignment with social status or social identity. Nonetheless, lack of fear does not mean a lack of continuity for the rebirth across each stage of different cycles. Be real with what you fear. Don't let the fear impact your decisions negatively for you to move to your desired stage. Isaiah 41 vs. 10 (KJV) provides comfort to know that the Lord our God that goes ahead of you and is with you, he will strengthen you, help you and uphold you with his righteous right hand.

Perceptivity and discernment are needed to overcome the challenges of fear. In your moments of hesitancy within the *Totally^U Career Cycle*, ask yourself why you are afraid to move to another stage? Your answer starts with the conversation you have with yourself about the source of your fear. Are they irrational? This is a key question to ask yourself in presensing and co-sensing.

Frenemies

It took my mother's death to retreat into two months of isolation, or "Monk Mode," to free myself from the repetitive cycle outside of myself. Self-isolation liberated me from friends and coworkers who claimed to mean well but sadly couldn't be trusted. This was a time to become more aware of what psychologists call my allies and adversaries in my work environment. Some of the ambivalent relationships were wonderful, while a few were not so much. Whether you are within the _Totally^U Drifter_, _Totally^U Defeater_, or _Totally^U Achiever_ stage, not everyone is trying to exploit you for your "it." So, when you find these people, who informally guide and mentor you, appreciate and hold on to them.

Some coworkers take their toll on you and are costly for your emotions, which can be a liability for your career progression. There are, however, other types of coworkers that need no explanation - frenemies. The most dangerous trait of these frenemies is they may display no hint of hypocrisy or envy. It is good to recognize them. The frenemies are your usual friend-of-a-friend or coworker you get along with and, overall, enjoy their company. Yet, these same people may look at you, hate your guts, and compete with you for no particular reason or perhaps your "it" factor. Whatever meaning frenemies place on the social definition of "It" is.

It can be your social standing within the organization. For instance, you don't even have to be within the _Totally^U Achiever_ stage; you will attract people after your "It." These shiny objects are the prestige and power that comes with your identity of society's definition of being successful. However, these are the people that may cut you down at virtually any opportunity.

Frenemies come in many guises. I have met the "Office Paparazzi" throughout the decades; the one who needs to capture everyone's story. The envious "Grudgers" who are jealous of your "It" and judge your ability and cringe at any celebration of your work successes. The "Know It All" who will pass a remark about everything you do. The "Gaslighters" inject their fears when evidence points to them being snubbed by feelings of inadequacy. The "Power Mad" who want more power for their own sake and the desire to prove they are the "boss" and heroine their role. Finally, there are the "Spoilers," who spill nothing more than negativity to retard your professional growth.

The stakes become even higher in a complex, revolving world in good ways and some wrong ways. Keeping someone around who is not really on your side often comes at a high cost. You might pick the "Office Paparazzi" to keep your workdays from becoming boring, with the need to make it more exciting. Or maybe you want to be in the loop to hear of any promotions or opportunities. To maintain your position with the pleasure of feeling superior, you become the Grudger out of a feeling of outrage, hurt, and disappointment in your professional life.

You will need these coworkers if you are on your way forward to find yourself within the say the *Totally^U Achiever* stage, and you will need them if you are on the way towards to a *Totally^U Drifter* stage. You will most definitely need them to get passed the *Totally^U Defeater* stage.

Within your career, you don't have to get along with everyone or force unnecessary interaction in the name of team spirit. The time you spend with these people can be emotionally expensive, and it is not psychologically healthy to do so. Know the purpose your frenemies serve. Skillfully navigate these relationships. So, be picky. Stop watering dead plants with some of these frenemies.

Most people I researched for this book on frenemies had at least one of these frenemies in their career or life. So, you can only be warned such professional associations come at a cost to your emotional life. The actual price of focusing on a family, friends, acquaintance, or colleagues who wears the sarcastic or narcissist cap could take time away from working on you becoming *TotallyU*. When another person's agenda can no longer control you, your state of mind flourishes. As a result, your highest point of contribution is discovered for your career and your purpose in the world.

Betrayal of Trust

———

Trust has a dark sibling.

The name is Betrayal.

The quality of the relationships formed in the organization is the basis for your feeling of belongingness and is central to your career survival. As you become more emotionally mature in your career, you place trust in the relationships you form along the way. The same currency that creates a relationship, trading of information, and confiding in the other person establishes that trust. Unfortunately, placing your trust in others is not a sure thing and not entirely safe. It is nothing like when you were firstborn.

During this time, you have no choice but to place your trust and life in your parent's hands. As a minimum, they provide your basic psychological needs—food and shelter. In addition, they provide love, comfort, security, and a sense of belonging at a deeper level.

Unfortunately, our 'All but One' society encourages others to become less trustworthy. Sadly, the actions and intentions of other people from jealousy, greed, and power can be disheartening. Few individuals relish the feeling of powerlessness in their work performance, as it opens up their vulnerability, and they risk the ability to form a relationship. However, making betrayal of that trust may be catastrophic or even life-threatening.

Regrettably, there is no guarantee that social contract will remain either as organizational resources decline and change, and promotion opportunities exist. As career professionals, we all pursue an agenda of self-interest in a competitive workplace to build accomplishment for ourselves and others. We attempt to control the impression others form of us in the process. We conform, make excuses, apologies, promote ourselves, practice flattery, favors, and association to protect our behaviors

Office political behavior is likely to rear its ugly head. When that relationship falls apart, regardless of our status in the organization, we feel let down and betrayed by our coworkers and employer. This connects betrayal with toxic work environments overall. I cannot count the number of times a career professional leaves such an environment they commonly describe where they felt they had lost a piece of their soul. A stressed environment will see this behavior, where the "Competitor" needs to win at all costs.

From various power bases, people around us will act differently. As a career professional within the $Totally^U$ Drifter, we may experience decreased job satisfaction and make excuses. $Totally^U$ Defeater individuals, already fragile, anxiety increases. We apologize and eventually quit. As a career $Totally^U$ Achiever, we may have reduced performance or practice flattery. Choosing the wrong people to trust, opening up, and sharing our vulnerability are used for coworkers' agendas. Some people are more politically "astute" than others to handle betrayal, but there is no escaping: it is a person-environment survival fact. The best asset we have is ourselves to figure out the emotions required at each stage to make shifts within the $Totally^U$ Career Cycle. To constantly reinvent at each professional stage, we will crave and seek to understand who we are as we learn to unlearn a new level of awareness of trust and betrayal.

.

Chapter 15: OperationU

O*perationU* is a simple plan. It is all about you.

It will open possibilities you never knew existed to do what you dream in your career. It brings about awareness to maximize your talent and capabilities for exponential growth and for self-transcendence to realize success in your professional life. As you may now have learned, your career reality is far more complex than merely finishing school and starting a job.

These are unquestioned convictions from beliefs developed. These feelings lay dormant inside and are suppressed over the years, impacting your current reality. These aren't something obvious yet profound. The control exerted through your current cognition in a complex and fragile work environment makes you mask, ignore, and hide your private thoughts and emotions.

It is worthwhile to revisit the *Totally^U Career Cycle*. You will appreciate this cycle as a more definitive way to validate where you stand in your professional life. Without placing labels, it represents you on a stage as an *Achiever, Drifter,* or *Defeater* at any point in your career. The *Totally^U Career Cycle* is a compass that represents your emotional state at each stage.

It is powerful because it helps you make better sense of yourself and your career reality in the most efficient way possible. The cycle starts with the premise that all aspects of a career's professional knowledge and experience have given partial truth to the individual. It then ties together all the elements of the subjective dimension of your interpersonal attributes or burners and other non-personal factors. Then, it consciously makes sense of an increasingly complex 21st-century organization to your current work reality. This is achieved through strategies to identify your emotional triggers and state of mind at work and by elaborating on intentionally organizing and engaging these emotional states to respond positively to any emotional stimulus.

After, the *Totally^U Framework* creates a map of your career's most significant interpersonal and non-interpersonal potential and acknowledges your survival within the *Totally^U Career Cycle*. You then have the freedom from the push-pull of your current state of mind, which helps bring alive what you want to experience and develop.

The goal so far is that by now, you will have figured out where you fall within the *Totally^U Career Cycle*. You have recognized the hidden patterns wrapped up in your ego, self-identity, passions, career ambitions, and the fixations gleaned from an organization's need to dominate profit and market share. This can evoke emotions that move you away from one thing and toward another where a frequency of matching and mismatching triggers your response. Knowing this calls for a state of operation.

OperationU integrates and synchronizes efforts to build an emotional operating system that leads to your desired future career state. It can adjust the demands of different work environments and modalities. A well-formed plan between thinking through and acting on your thoughts towards becoming *TotallyU* is your private inner experience and is therefore mutual to your work situation. *OperationU* therefore provides the tools to move through each level, bringing a generative shift in how you think, feel, respond, relate, and perform.

Whenever you experience any discomfort from organizational politics, coworkers, fear, or powerlessness, take a moment to notice what you are thinking and feeling. Don't bury or burn your feelings and the emotions you experience. Instead, own those aspects of your reality and leverage them for balance. Create an appreciation of your reality and state of mind on each "burner" in your current stage. No matter who you are, you can magnify your state of mind by being aware of your emotional triggers and response on each stage of the $Totally^U$ Career Cycle. Here, your state of mind becomes truly profound collectively with your personal and non-personal attributes.

The $Totally^U$ Framework intends to honor these dimensions wherever you're feeling underdeveloped and encourages you to embrace your emotional state as you move from one stage to another through the cycle. In undertaking OperationU, you alter distortions in your thinking pattern and test emotional resistance, eliciting your emotional self-defense mechanism. Rather than repairing what you feel is broken, the focus is to empower you to excel in your vision and dream about what is possible.

Moving towards becoming TotallyU is your unique inner experience and only applicable to you and your work situation.

To complete this state of operation depends on the current challenges in each stage and your level of urgency to either strengthen your existing position or gain a new stage. By upping your game and sensory awareness, you can identify and monitor your needs to achieve self-actualization. As a result, you can hatch a well-formed plan between thinking through and managing your thoughts as part of OperationU.

OperationU Plan

———

A s a well-educated and qualified individual, believe that you are correct and know that you can bring about your desired change. However, I do not promise it will be easy to understand what needs to be changed. Within *OperationU*, you are the person you've been waiting for. Unfortunately, no one else is coming to make you accountable. Many educated and qualified career professionals remain stuck within the *Totally^U Drifter* stage. They are often "muted" by organizational politics, micro-managers, and a workload that would require an eighteen-hour workday to complete.

The *Totally^U Defeater* career professional may have become dumb from lacking a voice and eventually loses their state of mind. The well-functioning *Totally^U Achiever* stage professional may not hurt or experience emotional discomfort. Still, they need to embrace emotional shift patterns to keep their compass aligned and continue to feel important.

This shift is within reach and possible because you are already an educated and qualified top performer who intelligently knows what you should not be settling for. Embrace a shift and watch career growth possibilities come to light. You are your best asset. To unlock the next stage of your career means you constantly examine your state of mind at each stage, as well as a willingness to unlearn and relearn. If you don't like the stage, you are at in your career, own up to it, restore your vision, and revive your passion for the job you look forward to every morning.

There will be times when you only need to adjust one of your interpersonal attributes or burners to get you where you want to go.

Another time, you may need to turn on all of them. Minor adjustments make a big difference to all that a career can bring. Listen to your aversion to fear, anger, stress, unpleasantness, intolerance, and "just had enough." These will provide a clue to your current state and help drive you to create a ferocious, resolved *OperationU* decision plan. It is time for you to confront areas where subtle passivity or even poor choices may have stifled your creativity.

When you learn about yourself and the stage you are in within the *Totally^U Career Cycle*, you'll experience a wide range of emotions. You may feel angry because, deep down, you are not where you think you should be in your career. Whether you are within the *Totally^U Drifter*, *Totally^U Defeater*, or *Totally^U Achiever* stage, you may never have envisioned being at that stage in your career. It can feel sad, or you may feel troubled and ashamed of your past jobs. Feeling fearful, afraid, and unsure of how to handle a career shift leads to blaming others and yourself for your past choices and decisions. Considering your career from a new perspective may leave you annoyed and perhaps overcome with sadness. Again, you may blame others in the past. However, moving to the desired stage is the only option for your career within the *Totally^U Career Cycle*. So, the solution is within reach. Take personal responsibility by owning your stage and reframing your thoughts to actualize your success.

Just like my seven-year-old self, who stood on my little stool behind the counter helping my Aunt Ty as we placed her customer's order, you can realize your worth. It was my first sense of feeling important, contributing to a significant role. It was magical. A true *aha*-moment of "*Yes, I have found my place.*" Some career professionals have not found their Damascus moment, their turning point, and life-changing instant, as they are yet to discover the importance of their careers' identity. *OperationU* shows you how to open up to being *TotallyU* and reposition your thoughts and emotions for self-actualization and self-worth.

In line with personal development, you map your career's most significant potential along with three progressive levels to become *TotallyU* at each stage. Each level will demand a different version of you and your role to manifest. Level one is where you own your present stage, take on your current role as an *Interrupter*, and examine current emotional challenges.

The other progressive level is where you reframe your thoughts in your identified stage, assuming the role of an *Awakener*. Finally, within the third level, as an *Actualizer*, you start to live out the script you have created for your career story, and with a reframed mind, you become the *Finisher* for reaching your desired stage. Only then, you are a different version of you to genuinely manifest meaningfulness, purpose, and importance.

Chapter 16: Own It

As well-intended as it may be, advice given by educational gurus can cause untold psychological damages. The different degrees of validity and their accuracy do not medicate the reality of our career delusion. Generations are misled about their career pathways, and as a result, throughout our careers, we give up complete authenticity to stay safe and sane on the job. We do this because we were not trained to skillfully address our emotions as they arise in our work environment.

In trying to limit or avoid these unpleasant work experiences, we evade the challenges to control our thoughts. Eventually, what we build to protect and insulate ourselves instead becomes incarcerated in our minds. We then become masters at shutting out the disappointment and constantly staying provoked in our current work conditions. We either stay with the same mindset, or it progressively gets worse. And our careers become tasteless, filled with indulgences to cover up its emptiness.

My only intent for you is to surrender to the stage you've been exposed to and notice the *Totally^U Career Cycle*. Owning your stage is the first level within the *Totally^U Framework*. Owning it means relinquishing all attempts to control your emotions at your identified stage and connecting to the deepest source of yourself to act from a *TotallyU* holistic stance. Once you have identified your stage, you have taken on the role of an *Interrupter* to own that stage.

As an *Interrupter*, your brain attempts to find balance. No peace of mind lives there when you are uncomfortable and curious. You first need to understand your interpersonal attributes and how they relate to you. Then you learn about the emotional trigger from your work experiences. As an *Interrupter*, your goal is to push all limits of your inner self to find and link the emotion with the event causing it. It starts with indirect private verbal conversations or talking to yourself about thoughts and feelings regarding "specific" times and events at your identified stage.

Challenge yourself with questions such as *"When was the first time I noticed and felt this way at work?"* With newfound awareness, you can respond to critical interpersonal clues that would have otherwise blocked your emotions. This awareness is a powerful source for guidance and direction as you advocate for your state of mind on your fresh path to your desired stage. The acts of selflessness when owning your stage can be experienced and not just described.

From a *TotallyU Framework*, owning a stage is an experience bigger than just what happens inside each of us individually. You come to understand how your identity is an illusion in which you know yourself. For instance, you cannot have a discontented work environment disappear or compare yourself to your coworkers objectively and open-mindedly unless you are personally non-judgmental, curious, and kind towards yourself. It can equally apply to your career journey, as your developmental growth sequence is dysfunctional or suboptimal.

To intentionally introduce yourself to the new you, in any state, means scanning your mental state every second of your workday to label and explore the associative feeling. Your emotions operate through your operating system, similar to a command-line interface. You are booting your emotional operating system to interact directly with all the triggers and requests for emotional response through interfacing with your work environment.

Your emotional operating system is the indirect instruction manual giving meaning and appraisal patterns of your emotions in your professional life that you may or may not already know. In the perpetuation's rebirth of cyclic existence, you need to fine-tune your attention with an open mind. Presencing allows your inner voice to interrogate the origins of the emotions to process and develop helpful inhibitions to handle those emotional disturbances as they happen, asking questions like *"How do I feel right now?"* Then, as you think about it and feel it, write it in a journal. It is a way to be profoundly honest with yourself about your unconscious emotions as they surface in black and white. You will see emerging patterns that give you the propulsion to say "yes" to the possibilities and create readiness to become *TotallyU*.

Once you look inwardly, conflict, confusion, and a completely disorganized state of mind are revealed. Fear of knowing your truth and anger at what you tolerated in your career will roam at will. If not careful, you mask your work experiences and emotions every day, and you build a shadow that follows you around to become the source of emotions for a different stage within the cycle. Failure to label your emotions will make it hard to link the trigger with the feelings correctly.

This can go wrong in two ways and centers on control. First, you perhaps inhibit all expression. You do nothing or say nothing and stop your emotions before they are consciously registered. There is the inability to control your actions, words, or impulses even when it gets you into trouble. Whether it be confronting or arguing with the paparazzi coworker or discussing the challenges with your boss. Or perhaps it is engaging in self-defeating disclosure and behaviors towards the person who is the source of your confusion. For instance, when Mark was vying for promotion in his accounting role, he may have experienced too much emotion and exaggerated the input of an innocent remark as a threat to the position and title he was after. The feelings and emotions he experienced is a gestalt of anger, not just tension for the continued survival of the *Totally^U Drifter* stage.

Repetition of your action is relevant. It becomes second nature as you pinpoint precisely where you are within the cycle and associate and identify with those disowned parts of yourself. Here, obtaining awareness of self-reality results in a "freedom from the "tug-of-war" of your desires, ambitions, and fixations. Liberation from the work environment's domination conquers greed, power, and delusion. It also nurtures the practice to suspend judgment, old habits of perception and thoughts, and allows you to connect with what's happening within you.

This is akin to the destruction and cessation of samsara and karmic activity, where the natural cycle of creation, maintenance, death and rebirth and a way of life are cyclic and one of growth. Here, the Totally^U path to ownership does not differ from the Buddhist Paths to liberation. The 'self' does not exist as a permanent integral, autonomous being within an individual existence, but a transient experience. For example, liberation insight may become predominant, recognizing and accepting the anatta doctrine of your patterns, beliefs, and habits, and in seeking understanding for greater wisdom, you give up everything to own your *Stage*. Your past guiding principles or core values trigger and fuel your thoughts, actions, and behaviors.

And this same experience is how career professionals shut out their disappointment. They sign in to work and leave their souls at home. Many are physically present yet mentally absent. Instead, they would rather collect a paycheck without physically showing up, develop temporary amnesia and remember only on Sunday or Friday. Career professionals do not own their situations at this stage.

When present, it is not unusual for one to walk through the doors of their work environment like the walking dead, wondering if it will ever be possible to find the love, vitality, and excitement in a job and experience the joy and peace of being accomplished. It is times like this that you need to remember that there is a difference between where you are *now* and where you want to be. This realization involves asking, "How does this stage I have identified within the *Totally^U Career Cycle* affect my current professional life?"

As a career professional, it doesn't matter if you are within the *Totally^U Drifter, Totally^U Defeater*, or the *Totally^U Achiever* stage. What you do next makes a difference as you move forward. Only when you can go back to your personal "burners," acknowledge, and then gauge them will you feel deeply "calibrated" with yourself. This is part of becoming *TotallyU*. Remaining present and owning your stage connects you in a way necessary to enact meaningful shifts and gauge your emotional health without you having to lose. If you want to see how challenging and the reward of "owning it" really is, try to live it for a week.

Personally, getting in "Monk-mode" invades my thoughts to connect to a deeper source of knowledge, and not only my beliefs about my attributes. It was not an intellectual deficit or the reason I developed an imposter syndrome, but an internal representation of my childhood, stemming from an abusive household and a misunderstanding of the source of my not speaking that needed to be interrupted.

When you confront yourself, it gives you a sense of righteousness towards your career purpose instead of becoming overwhelmed to sink you into despair or depression. You listen on your stage, and as an *Interrupter*, with your mind and heart wide open. You are present to confront your fears, bias, powerlessness, and certainty of identity in the workplace.

In the value of Buddhism's idea of impermanence, all things constantly occur, "moment to moment", and disappear once they have originated. As of today, bring alive what you want to experience and nurture wherever you feel underdeveloped to gain what was yours in a career with a clear-sightedness. Don't spend your career stuck or held captive in a pattern. But, on the other hand, don't hide from the truth you need to hear, either. You are better off confronting your truth than being in denial.

As a gentle reminder, whether you are within the *Totally^U Drifter*, *Totally^U Defeater* or a *Totally^U Achiever* stage, the relationships you have formed at work are waiting to benefit from you not recognizing or concealing your emotions.

Chapter 17: Reframed

==

One of the many things I became obsessed with while at a *Totally*^{U} *Drifter* stage was focusing on what I am in my professional life. Unfortunately, my mother's passing to cancer created a breakthrough that reshaped my thinking. A complete vision awakened to guide me to my desired destination. It could be performance feedback that suddenly gives a mirror that leads to devising a compelling and exciting strategy for some of you.

First, I recognized I had a thorn in my flesh all these years, just like Paul, the apostle. I had to generate sufficient emotional energy to trust God more and let my faith work in my current way of thinking, feeling, and acting. Then, I reframed my emotion to come to terms with the reality of owning my stage. Finally, I integrated my head and heart to move from and towards what needed to happen within me without interference. My mother's death caused me to reframe my assessment of myself. A ferocious resolve of a decision, I had no choice but to assume the role of an *Awakener*, the second level of the *Totally*^{U} *Framework*.

My *Awakener* role was heightened because of my early years of development. In the early years, I lost my sense of speaking, and the section of my brain that handled sensory information was rewired to hearing. *Awakeners* are powerful observers and listeners because they know that the reality of trade-offs means they can't possibly pay attention to everything. They listen deliberately and actively for what others do not explicitly state. They read between the lines and listen for what others do not hear at the periphery by listening to what is not said. In doing so, they avoid distraction from extraneous noise, such as loud voices that may pull them in many directions.

Awakeners must learn to resist distractions and keep their focus. Blocking the noise and controlling the signal is not new, and the concept has been around for years. As listeners, we magnify certain interesting information and filter out other information.

When we have a sensory experience, even when there may be nothing inherently wrong about the behavior, in our mind, it is not the experience we dislike but rather our actual response to it. So, when reframed, the meaning given to the response is to cause an "affective" behavior by asking you to leave the content the same and change the meaning of the behavior in that same context. And as people tend to attach only one meaning to each sensory experience, the behavior is reframed.

Reframing is an undeniably valid way of looking at the world. Flexible thinking about something is an integral part of understanding. If you're not using your language to create and naturally empower your beliefs, then you will be the victim of negative thoughts pushing you in the wrong direction.

If I were to ask three career professionals at different stages within the *Career Cycle*, they would attach different meanings to the same external event. Asking someone within the *Totally^U Defeater* stage about their professional growth within their present work environment, the response would be similar to "There are too many problems here, and they can't seem to get their act together." A *Totally^U Achievers* stage individual's response may be, "This is a dynamic company with a proportionately risk-reward relationship, and it is remarkable working for them." Therefore, every sensory experience in the world and every behavior is appropriate in some context.

We see these emotions differently when we change the meaning to capture and decide what to do about it. Sandy, the janitorial worker, is a powerful example of how an individual views and reframes her work environment. A look at things from a different perspective gives us choices.

With choices, you can start telling stories to yourself, which are created with possibilities of things you didn't know at the start of the process. Reframing the content from your emotions is simply disrupting the pattern of that story to give you more choices. All along, within the $Totally^U$ Career Cycle, you've had a story, but your emotional state drove you to forget to tell yourself. These stories are needed to continue your journey around the cycle. I am not suggesting that you change as you script your story. This would be like telling you to change your self-identity in an already complex organization and other subsystems in which you carry out *OperationU*. Also, if you consciously alter your thoughts, you may end up removing or altering powerful mental signs of progress or metaprograms that influence other thought processes.

You may have your entire career crashing down or being at the mercy of your own personal and professional life. Yet, every learning moment is an organic opportunity to shed an old self to showcase the new. There is limited room in your career and on earth, and you need to fill the space with stories to make you feel accomplished with a healthy state of mind. It boils down to realizing the things you appreciate with optimism, not your discord. If it means taking risks, keep trying, however long it takes.

Let's not forget Kentucky Fried Chicken's (KFC) founder, Harland David Sanders. He patented his frying chicken method at sixty-three years old and is now the international franchise KFC brand. So, every step taken on this journey is an opportunity to celebrate your story, and the only person who can be accountable is *TotallyU*.

When you tell a story and reframe it into a more attractive position than where you are now, you are closer to becoming *TotallyU*. The stories you create are to align and not escape your identity as you move into a state of importance to achieve career success with a clear mind. Recognize yourself in the story and the survival skills to navigate the organizational landscape of your emotional map. Absorb the possibility of what is new. Identify yourself in the story of actions you need to take now to keep striving. However, the reframing process is, in part, a process of learning to see yourself in the narrative in a positive or constructive light.

There is something I want you to know. You had that capability long before you thought you did. You are only reclaiming what has been dormant inside of you. One courageous step leads to rich insights that give your story energy to come to reality. To continue your story amidst uncertainty, you still need to continually remind yourself of your career journey before the collision of personal and organizational fit occurred. As you embrace shifts, change is challenging when you tend to believe and reinforce your existing emotions, feel what you want to feel, and believe what you want to believe.

While this can be a good thing, the career you want is all a thought. It is about being honest and not making any excuses for the professional life you have within the *Totally^U Defeater*, *Totally^U Drifter*, or *Totally^U Achiever* stage. Being an *Awakener*, you must be congruent in nonverbal analogs to have the reframe be effective. By giving yourself the flexibility to change the way you feel and think, you are forcing yourself to dig deeper and sometimes work with scarce resources. Open-mindedness and focus will make you creative in your pursuit of being *TotallyU*.

A reframed environment could have consequences for curiosity. When you consume information, you are challenged to question the assumptions and validity of the information. It can frustrate and be difficult, driving you to seek knowledge about various content. For instance, to figure out the *Totally*^{U} *Defeater* stage means that something is hidden. The invisible compels you to learn about what you don't know, what you couldn't think of, and what you couldn't conceive. You are required to consider what you never understood or entertained to push you towards a *Totally*^{U} *Achiever* stage or push you down to a *Totally*^{U} *Drifter* stage.

Your mindset or mental force is needed to know what to frame and accommodate, and you explore your motivation for reframing when you want to identify with actually being accomplished.

Do you adapt or accommodate to fit the organization? Your new story may sound like imagery. One thing that remains is the truth in your script. The embellished version gives you the courage and energy to better actualize the outcome of the story you create for the core message to become *TotallyU*. Your external forces, egos, friends, trust, betrayal, and social media can generate a sense of inertia of your confirmation biases. The need to shift to an entirely new stage with a unique identity again is up to you. Evaluate the things and people in your life, promote, demote, or terminate.

As I progressed through the *Totally*^{U} *Career Cycle*, my truth was in changing to reach my desired outcome. Following interviews, where I was told I was overqualified, I reinterpreted the results to be more constructive. I replaced them and reframed them with empowering language, "It is the hiring company's loss, not mine. My work ethics, skills and aptitude would have enhanced their outcome." Being present, I noticed the questions I was asking myself. If they were negative emotional responses, I replaced them with positive questions. A technique I practice is to sport a rubber band at all times as a reminder to correct my behavior. Each time I experience a negative emotional response to an event trigger, I pull the rubber band to remind myself of the story I am creating for the continuity of my career journey.

Transition is hard, but telling your positive story is more attractive than where you are now. Your stories will ease the path forward.

Chapter 18: Actualize it

⸻

Is living a clear state of mind important? Yes, it's all significant for your success at work. It is everything. The *Totally^U Framework* has so far helped you to understand and explore the alignment of your state of mind with meaningfulness by connecting your work and interpersonal-related issues. For faith in *OperationU*, much has to be given, and much more is required to move forward. But it is just the beginning.

We all struggle with something within our work environment in our careers. The emotions you experience at work do not differ from what others undergo. Career professionals within the *Totally^U Achiever* stage may agonize with ego, whereas others within the *Totally^U Drifter* dreads fear, and the *Totally^U Defeater* individuals may have frustrations. Some employers are not sensitive to people's needs and are not willing to change their plans at a moment's notice. Thus, the more you look at your story maturely, the more you are bringing it to perfection and acting out the performance of your account.

This should motivate you to become a successful individual in your professional life. However, it only happens when you understand your final role as *Finisher* of your career story within the *Totally^U Framework*. When the ink dries on the paper, we all need to make sure it is from our pen for our personal growth. You are who you are, and no one can write your script. You are the author and finisher.

Wanting differs from choosing. There is limited room in your life—flip-flops hit harder when you get older, and some life events deliberately throw you off course. So many people have had the experience of their career blossoming when suddenly tragedy strikes. Through self-awareness or enlightenment, you realize the "garbage" that takes up space in your life. You never unload when you stop at any loading dock, so your story never takes any form or directness. Always too busy with the past and predicting the future doesn't leave room for meaningfulness. But, once you've identified the things that got you to where you are today within the $Totally^U$ *Drifter*, $Totally^U$ *Defeater*, $Totally^U$ *Achiever* stage, and as you own that stage, you reframe the emotions to actualize the end goal.

Whatever your intention when deliberately reinventing yourself, it is up to you to feed-forward your desires. All along, you have accepted your career fallacy and have gotten comfortable being uncomfortable. The other monsters in the closet fear joining the force against you, not acting. That is why the third and final level of the $Totally^U$ *Framework* is where I advocate for you to act as a *Finisher*.

Do not delude yourself about the inner work that you really must take to get into motion. The same distinction arises with people deciding to change for the better. Finishing your story starts with distinguishing between what you want in your career and how you choose to reach the next stage. If you make the wrong choice, you may fall into a different stage of the $Totally^U$ *Career Cycle*. Even if it is not a quantum leap, focusing on what is correct and building on those "rights" will get you to the desired stage. Such as gauging your burners.

Instead of fast, automatic information processing, you recognize and adjust your emotions and behaviors for constant adaptation. You psychologically flex your mind so you can deal with almost anything your work environment throws at you. You will then solidify new emotional experiences from owning and reframing your state of mind to integrate with the new habits formed. Therefore, you create an action plan that will allow you to continue representing your values and pursuing your standing within the *Totally^U Career Cycle* in the face of distractions and obstacles.

Actualizing it means integrating the disparate aspects of the self then negotiating with separate parts to achieve resolution of any internal conflict, so it fits ecologically into your lifestyle. Finally, nurture and celebrate new behaviors in response to emotional triggers from consensing and presencing to being a *Finisher*.

Keep in mind to always strive to discover positive intentions into actionable outcomes to actualize your stage. For example, suppose you develop a thought habit where you think you are not good enough. Here, you will be bound to create a fear of being exposed and judge yourself as a failure that often causes frustration and leads to negative behaviors. The pull-away behaviors from moving away from unwanted mental experiences almost instantly feel good. Emotions arising out of fear, sadness, anger, frustration, depression, and boredom can help you operate efficiently and safely in your work environment. So, if you decide to ask your boss for a raise in pay, fear shows up, but you get away from the fear when you ask and you receive a positive response. Although "asking" does not feel good at that moment, it releases the fear and that feels good.

Any thoughts that aren't pushing you forward are only meant to hold you back. Thank your unconscious mind for your ideomotor response. Fully imagine trying your alternatives where previously it would have been a behavior. Ask your unconscious mind to give you a signal when there are new alternatives. Put a time limit on the request to try out the other options to determine the effectiveness and availability. Make sure it is entirely comfortable and accept the entire process. Examine the unconscious mind for any visible sign, like a facial expression reflecting the internal sensation of your emotional response. As you endure the work environment and make it to the end of a workday, you go home and figure out what in the world you should feel. And because life is unpredictable, you can become exhausted from controlling these thoughts for your career outcomes.

Unique aspects of your interpersonal attributes conflict because of different perceptions and beliefs. It is easiest to spend your energy controlling your image than to be vulnerable for a moment, as you risk rejection or retaliation and falling into another undesirable stage of the *Totally^U Career Cycle.*

Your current state and your future state needs should both want the same thing—to embrace and merge as an accomplished, successful career professional. You will no longer take a position and not do the job from not having a clear state of mind. Take as long as you need to regenerate parts of yourself. Put everything we have discussed so far into perspective this time. Be personally involved.

You will put the weight on your shoulders and be responsible and present. Trying to embrace a shift is a great place to start. Be mindful of emotions and triggers from the past and reach for the possibilities ahead. Maybe the last time you tried to speak up at work, you were reprimanded or fired. Perhaps the last time you confided in a coworker, they betrayed you. If you are late in your career and it has no meaning, now is not the time to be holding your wound while you stitch your scars. Indulge in your vulnerability that the past teaches us to camouflage.

This entire book is about self-discovery, and you may feel disconnected from knowing your career status and place within the *Totally^U Career*

Cycle. You may feel you do not have it all together, but you can add exponential value to your career progression in incremental steps. You will have faith in the past and hope in the future instead of repeatedly pacing, hoping to experience a shift as your professional life draws to an end. If you are a career professional who is already accomplished and do not feel success, up the need to take big paces.

Revisiting social and self-identity, we try to prove to ourselves with various self-proclamations where we never feel fulfilled. So, we seek validation from systems and people who place little value or importance on us as individuals. Our reality is the only accurate indicator from our actions expressed from ignorance, apathy, and self-sabotage, coupled with our self-interest.

During your role as *Finisher,* if you come across situations and people that make you feel you have to validate yourself, run away! Pay attention to the work situations and people who make your heart palpitate. The unhealthy energies require many dispensations needed to handle. Being a *Finisher* is about your highest level of self.

With the conditioned existence of *OperationU,* you eventually control the emotional process, slowly and effortlessly, with concentration and complete attention to finishing. Everything from owning your stage, reframing your thoughts within your stage, and actualizing your desired stage with a new effort. This is your first state of renunciation through conscious attention as a successful and accomplished career professional with a clear state of mind.

Chapter 19 Triumphs Over Triggers

All journeys are unique, and mine began with me not saying my first words until I was seven years old, growing up in a dysfunctional family and poverty, and walking off jobs because I care more about the people than the process and politics. The disturbance along the journey causes an awakening. So, like many, mine is a unique tale with twists and turns that caused shifts and gave my life meaning and purpose.

Looking back, some of my stories bring tears to my eyes. Some rejuvenate my soul and put a smile on my face. Some strengthen me. I have realized that other people's stories draw me in and intrigue me throughout my journey. Those "one pair of ears" that I disliked as a child were like a one-hundred and eighty-degree antenna that I used to my advantage. I developed those muscles to listen to their journey and my career expedition to create an awesome story of becoming "*TotallyU.*" This is what we know so far.

Everyone is already within the *Totally^U Career Cycle*, yet may not realize their stage's specifics. Some journeys are like a divided fork with multiple roads between all three stages. Without pretense, you may be too proud to think you have total control over a career that continues to erupt with explicable disturbances in your own state of mind.

Regardless, it forms a powerful story similar to other career professionals. Some stories leave teary eyes, and some may leave a smile for the sacrifices and challenges that took you to the stage of a *Totally^U*

Achiever, Totally^U Defeater, or *Totally^U Drifter* stage. The merging of our paths inspires others to dream not about a necessary need for change but a want to change. Most people I have met have had some sort of defeat, or they end up walking without defeat. There is no ground rule for solving the dilemmas of the stage you are in emerging within *the TotallyU Deep Space.* So lay down your ego, heal your wounds from broken work relationships and find your purpose on earth that is appreciated.

Feed forward is a two-way conversation between you and yourself wanting to help your former self to the new you. Not only will it help you win the race, but it will also help you manage better the shifts necessary for your state of mind instead of premature evaluations. Rooted in deep religious belief, I found my happiness is not to worry, maybe just a minor concern. As Paul, the apostle, articulates, "Do not be anxious about anything, but in every situation, by prayer and petition, with thanksgiving, present your requests to God. The peace of God, which transcends all understanding, will guard your hearts and your minds in Christ Jesus" (Philippians 4:6 KJV).

Living in a fast-paced world, we have joined humanity to figure out the reason for a cyclical pattern of our careers. Whenever my patience was tested instead of premature evaluations, I learned to shut out the noise and became acutely mindful of the energy entering my space. I gave total disregard to the psychophysiological processes of the work environment—a critical intermediate causal pathway linking economic, social, and political structures to health and illness.

We spend most of our adult lives working. With science, our life expectancy has stretched and expanded and hence so has our working life. Those years fill with joy, and trials quickly pass by. While we spend most of our years working, there is more to life and our career than fitting on a cycle. When we can't engage in our career to a high level of importance, the focus may shift to what we're left with—that is our self. During this stage, the self is the most important aspect to protect. We find out we are the ones we wait on to show up all along.

Go into a *Monk Mode* if you need to, so you can break down your movements from distractions and confront questions you may never want to have answered. Get comfortable spending time with yourself and silence. Then, as you think it, write it down and meditate on it; each time you revisit and repurpose those experiences, this is a demonstrative response to an emotional trigger. These are some of the deep-rooted emotions that buried your hopes, dreams, and aspirations within the *Totally^U Drifter, Totally^U Defeater,* and the *Totally^U Achiever* stage.

Unfortunately, the map is not the territory, and you can confuse perception with reality. To live a life of authenticity, not what you perceive a *TotallyU Achiever* stage is and assume that it would mean success. Before now, what was once impaired emotional sight becomes self-awareness that lets in more light as time passes. The path along life's journey is to regenerate, feel authentic as you survive and recalibrate, and act the same way on the outside regardless of how you feel on the inside and irrespective of your work environment. This is especially so if you are a neurotic person who tends to become fired up by psycho-social organizational triggers.

Part of the *Totally^U Framework* is connecting with your spirituality, family, and work. It is a critical component in self-definition that often gets overlooked when triggers triumph over your careers and you act out your calling. The eternal truth substantiates your truth by the supreme being you worship. Your spirituality is the indirect instruction manual that comes to you when you are born to provide you with guidance and direction. Surrender can become necessary on the path to figuring out career meaning and purpose. Letting go and letting in can make a difference profoundly. You surrender to strip ego, greed and wants versus your needs, and as you make your journey, you become more aware of who you are when all else fails. Your divine creator wants you to achieve and attain your potential to walk on the right path. So, you can contribute to society and connect to serving others and yourself.

People are happy to have a job, but many of them no longer feel their workplace is a second home. Regrettably, career professionals are forced to accommodate with uncomfortable environments. Therefore, the trials and tribulations within the *Totally^U Career Cycle* are to test your very own existence, hope, and faith. Spiritual and religious beliefs influence your work-related values. Work-related values are thought prompts in your Supreme Divine Plan. This is the blueprint to control your emotions and to live and respond to these triggers that are authentic to who you are. The ultimate source of authority to do so is found inside. Approaching work as a calling, we have greater work and life satisfaction, more commitment to our profession, greater self-identity, clarity, and better use of problem-focused coping.

There comes a greater vocational self-clarity and attributed greater importance to careers. The salient difference between avoidance coping and those with other work approaches and an appreciation of a divine plan exists. With these components, you will less likely be concerned about sacrifices that accompany your career and accept duties that go beyond the job description.

Without deep sealed faith, searching for a place within the *Cycle* leaves you more undecided and uncomfortable in your career and lowers self-clarity. Engaging in work because it satisfies some interests rather than a means of getting a paycheck does not facilitate an adaptive approach to coping with inter-state conflict. Choosing an organization with cultural values that promote your experience of transcendence through the work process can facilitate your sense of being connected to others in a way that provides feelings of completeness and joy.

With biblical teachings and spiritual music to restore my equilibrium from work environmental stimuli, I became more of the person God wants me to be compared to what society wants me to become or a social system label within the confines of an organization. Triumph over triggers can be fostered by organizations that promote workplace mental health through spirituality and emotional wellness.

Chapter 20: Docked

———

Agrowing center-periphery labor market structure in Denmark, Iceland, Norway, and Sweden promotes job quantity, quality, and inclusiveness. This resonates with the *Totally*^{U} *Framework*. These countries perform better than those focusing predominantly on market flexibility and adaptability to create high-quality jobs in more dynamic environments that make working conditions more accessible for people to combine work, care, and social responsibilities. For the career professional, attaining control may be a way of minimizing or setting limits on risk and uncertainty.

Control gives you predictability, feelings of ownership for your job, and expectations of what might happen within a toxic or conducive organization. For example, a *Totally*^{U} *Achiever* stage career professional with control expects a less negative outcome than a *Totally*^{U} *Drifter* individual without control. The psychological sense of ownership is an integral part of the employee's relationship with the organization. Our true stage's fundamental choices and discovery are more important than our work environment. It shows that heightened awareness determines the heights that we reach and the contributions that we make to the organization and to society.

The experiences of career professionals within the *Totally*^{U} *Career Cycle* show that nothing in our career is left out. A challenge for psychosocial work environments is where the working conditions "get under your skin" and alter your embodiment, leading to non-performance and the development of subcultures. This is a two-way street. Not only does the work environment alter your mind and the body, but your cognitions and emotions also alter how you experience your working conditions. From a psychological perspective, an unconscious process is embodied while bypassing consciousness.

We may protest why we are within the *Totally*^{U} *Drifter, Totally*^{U} *Defeater*, and a *Totally*^{U} *Achiever* stage without realizing that these trials and tribulations enable us to improve our emotional agility and faith. Many successful professionals have experienced some kind of childhood trauma throughout their life prior to entering the *Totally*^{U} *Career Cycle*. Some were sexually molested, poor, or came from dysfunctional homes. Now a world-famous Motivational Speaker, Nick Vujicic was born with no limbs. Andrea Bocelli is a tenor, musician, writer, and music producer born with congenital glaucoma and later suffered other injuries that left him blind. Yet, he continues to have sold-out concerts globally. Richard Branson of Virgin Group has dyslexia, a learning disability. Franklin Roosevelt, United States 32nd President-Elect four times was struck by polio that left him with paralyzed legs.

A moment of appreciation should not be what happened to me instead of what is happening *to* me. If we can move through challenges at each stage, we will emerge stronger and wiser as we progress through the *Totally*^{U} *Career Cycle*. Our individual experiences within the *Totally*^{U} *Defeater, Totally*^{U} *Drifter* and *Totally*^{U} *Achiever* stage prepare us to make choices to find our purpose. Greek Philosopher Aristotle expresses these values that "Excellence is never an accident. It is always the result of high intention, sincere effort, and intelligent execution; it represents the wise choice of many alternatives—choice, not chance, determines your destiny."

I have seen the occupation that God has given to us to keep us occupied. In time, he connects us to our careers without gaining or losing our state of mind. Every station docked prepares us to experience before the travel can move on to bear the challenges of a career with dignity and grace and make the best of our circumstances.

The constant self-reflection and the acquisition of knowledge for the alignment with family, faith, and spirituality are unique to each of us within the *Totally^U Career Cycle*. You can acquire the tools and knowledge to shift within the *Totally^U Career Cycle*. But knowledge is only relevant when it leads to the deep-seated actions of our newfound awareness of our faith. This gives us the belief that carrying out work not by chance but by choice will endure our work environments. As you gain more strength in your faith, you will compromise with what you want and what you do not wish for. This level of certainty develops confidence, and you become more likely to tolerate your work environment. Remember, as you reflect, you develop an understanding of what needs to change and how you handle the *Achiever, Drifter*, or *Defeater* stage you are within.

By controlling our emotional triggers, we learn to forge our paths with confidence and to become successful in our careers. We need to adapt when breaking away from the undesired stage once identified. This opens possibilities, and we awaken to our current reality of the ideal career we now yearn to achieve. We can envisage our career with a clear state of mind.

Chapter 21: Anchored Safely

———

Although our work environments may be quite different, we all want the same thing on the journey to our destined careers. We need to develop skills of reflection, perspicacity, and clarity to support us through the stages of the *Totally^U Career Cycle*. However, these are not set-in-stone as there are times; when we feel the tide will never change in our professional life. Throughout history, we have seen successful people from humble beginnings and diverse backgrounds that rest on the power of the same principle of commitment, persistence, resilience, and responsibility of the *Totally^U* concept. They overcome work challenges to experience connectedness and fulfillment in spirituality, family, and work. It shows that it is not so much about the work environments we find ourselves in. It is the outcome of our actions within the *Totally^U Career Cycle* to pursue meaning in our professional life.

The *TotallyU* concept is intentionally restricted to how the career professional experiences and responds to their work-related environment. Our state of mind is evolving. If not careful, we are held captive to our own minds. As you pursue your desired stage, you either step forward into faith or step back into safety to have the career you have never had. The test and trials within the *Totally^U Career Cycle* help you develop your perseverance. We should allow space for this season in our professional lives because that is where we build our faith. As when our root is strong, we can sustain any wind.

Our creator uses renewed faith to help us find our purpose in our career and not lose our existence on earth. One thing that remains constant as we change jobs, and our emotional state is the presence of our divine creator. A lack of relationship thereof can leave us in a daze, confused, stuck, egotistical, and perhaps in a fight-or-flight mode from the unpleasantness and intolerance of our professional life.

However, we are surrounded by more noise and distraction than ever before that easily triggers our emotions. In a fast-paced world, silence makes us weary where it drives us to a place where we ask ourselves, *Is this all there is to work?* This is why achieving an optimal frequency of spirituality, family, and work requires being in tune with ourselves to block the noise around us and listen. Stillness in co-sensing and presencing is important as we become cognitive of what should happen within us through our divine creator. The ability to listen allows us to perform in our roles as *Interrupters, Awakeners,* and *Finishers.*

For a moment, hold off on emotional triggers from what is happening in your work environment. Focus your mind on being more receptive to the voice of your divine creator. Embody the thoughts as a reminder that you can do and face all things through Christ who strengthens you. Likewise, anchor in the safety of prayer. Pray for strength to endure. Pray for things and the people in your work environment who are causing the situation to trigger your emotions. "It may be helpful to pray for the self first before you go to work, for God to search you because he knows your heart; Try you and know your anxieties" (Psalm 139: vs 23 KJV). Recognize your feelings are just visitors. Let them come and go as the root of suffering psychologically within the organization is attachment to the emotions that are causing it.

Pray throughout your career journey as well. Each day, you get up and go to work, not knowing what you will face. Not knowing the monsters and to, deal with what is on your burners. Before you go to work, ask your creator to appeal to your frenemies, micromanager bosses, plead your cause against those who strive with you; "Fight against those who fight against you" (Psalm 35: 1- 3 KJV).

On your way to work, pray to know the weaknesses identified on your burners. To deal with the anxiety of knowing your fears, ego, and social identity. "Ask God to deal with you for your name's sake, for his mercy to deliver you." (Psalm 109 KJV). At nights, when reflecting on work, "pray to dress the wound of those who you come across daily as though it were not serious, ask that there be peace when there is no peace". (Jeremiah 6:14 KJV). Through persistence and deep actions rooted in your faith, your prayers will be heard and answered by your divine creator. With God, through this assurance, I have found strength. Continuously pray to be removed from the environment that weakens your mind to becoming *TotallyU*.

Sometimes we have to choose to lose because we are protected by our divine creator. However, not everything we lose is a loss. Even when we think we are all together, life is not always easy. No matter what we face, there is hope. God is always faithful. Understand that our strength cometh from God. For instance, ego is removed when you anchor in faith, yet awareness of self-identity and passion is found in your purpose. This is what is meant when they say you are grounded. Believe, and you will have more tolerance to manage your emotions as you walk by faith and not by feelings. Once you believe long enough, you will be amazed at what God can do.

God reaches us no matter what stage we are within the *Totally^U Career Cycle*. Instead of relying on the organization for your state of mind, you can depend on your spirituality to become resilient and fulfill your responsibility to stay persistent and committed at each stage of the *Career Cycle*. It also involves taking a personal risk by owing, framing, and actualizing your desired stage. Risk trusting God to take matters of your state of mind into his own hands, and risk having faith before having your questions answered. In the end, it is worth the risk of waiting on God to see a breakthrough in the right-person-environment fit—an amazing story of your professional life when your ship is anchored.

To put it differently, becoming *TotallyU* is about breaking the hold your mind has over your every moment, every experience, and every interaction.

When we get beyond the mind's constant habituation, it's thought patterns, fears, projections, ruminations, ramblings and self-talk is considered through the lens of our self-identity and our ambitions. Then we experience a state of mind in a direct, "spiritual" way. This is massively liberating. Wisdom comes through struggles and sorrows, and pain. And so, in the fullness of time, it is living the real, not the ideal. It is a reaffirmation of who you are and what is your calling in this world, and when you connect at a spirituality level, you can anchor safely in your professional life.

God took me around the ocean when I was really going to the next harbor. I am still on a voyage with my career as it constantly evolves and grows. I know God will respond to the faith of my commitment, persistence, resilience, and responsibility to him first. When my ship is docked and anchored, I find solace knowing I was the dumb girl who used her silence to surface loudly, inspire others, and run loud with a clear state of mind intellectually.

Applying the principles of *OperationU* within the *Career Cycle*, grounded in your faith, family, and moral values produces a clear state of mind to approach work that awaits you beyond your imagination. For example, suppose you lose a job but find yourself in the process. The old has gone. The new is here. You have become *TotallyU*.

TotallyU is **a** superpower. TotallyU is **your** superpower, and one you deserve, as you come to the end of your career pursuit, with a clear state of mind.

Don't miss out!

Visit the website below and you can sign up to receive emails whenever Gaile G. Sweeney publishes a new book. There's no charge and no obligation.

https://books2read.com/r/B-A-EPSS-RHHTB

BOOKS 2 READ

Connecting independent readers to independent writers.

Also by Gaile G. Sweeney

A Career Professional's State of Mind in the Pursuit of Meaning
TotallyU: A Source of Truth

About the Author

Gaile Sweeney, MBA, MPH, PMP, NLP is a Neuro Transformational Career and Life Coach, Speaker, and Author who has helped support countless people transform their personal and professional lives via her signature breakthrough coaching products. You can find out more about Gaile and sign up for the newsletter at gailesweeney.com

Read more at https://gailesweeney.com/.

About the Publisher